Forgiven and Free: Breakii

A Year Long Bible Study Focused on Second Chances

A Year Long Bible Study, A Journey of Faith, Forgiveness, and Second Chances!

Written By: David Phillips | Brand 316, Inc

Forgiven and Free: Breaking the Chains! A Year Long Bible Study Focused on Second Chances

Written, Content Created and Owned by David Phillips. Bible Verses Used From NIV unless otherwise noted.

David Phillips
Brand 316, Inc
727 North Waco Ave Suite 290
Wichita, KS 67203
www.brand316.org

ISBN: 9798334146983
Imprint: Independently published

Forgiven and Free: Breaking the Chains!
A Year Long Bible Study Focused on Second Chances

Table of Contents

Brand 316 Inc www.brand316.org 727 North Waco #290 Wichita KS 67203 (316) 247-2050

Brand 316 Inc www.brand316.org 727 North Waco #290 Wichita KS 67203 (316) 247-2050
Content Created and Owned by David Phillips | Do Not Duplicate nor Copy | All Rights Reserved

Brand 316 Inc www.brand316.org 727 North Waco #290 Wichita KS 67203 (316) 247-2050

ABOUT THE AUTHOR– DAVID PHILLIPS

David Phillips's journey is a testament to resilience, faith and the transformative power of second chances. Born into a family deeply rooted in Christian ministry, his father, Dr. Keith Phillips, founding World Impact, an inner-city ministry and his grandfather co-founding World Vision, David's heart for those in need was cultivated from a young age. David is a dynamic and results-oriented executive with a passion for entrepreneurship and social impact projects.

David was arrested by federal agents in 2017, facing charges (18 U.S. Code § 1958 - Use of interstate commerce facilities in the commission of murder-for-hire) that would forever alter his life. David maintained his innocence and refused to consider a plea deal that required him to admit to something he did not do, yet offer a significant sentence reduction. Through a tumultuous legal battle marked by injustice and corruption, David found himself incarcerated, navigating the complexities of the criminal justice system firsthand.

In prison, amidst the darkness and despair, David discovered a profound relationship with Christ that transcended the confines of his cell. Immersed in prayer, Scripture, and a renewed purpose to serve others, he experienced God's presence and guidance in the most unlikely of places. Despite the challenges and dangers of life inside, David became a beacon of hope, advocating for justice and assisting fellow inmates with legal matters, securing the early release of several, including himself.

As the Founder and President of Brand 316, Inc, David has pioneered a scalable Christian prison ministry aimed at nationwide implementation. Through comprehensive 52-week training programs he focuses on total reintegration training for inmates released emphasizing personal, professional, and spiritual development. David's commitment to providing the tools needed for success is reflected in the strategic partnerships he has cultivated with businesses, churches, and individuals to ensure immediate employment, mentorship, and acceptance for Brand 316 members upon release.

Prior to his work with Brand 316, David founded a digital marketing firm that quickly became a prominent player in the industry. Through his leadership, the company achieved double-digit annual growth, serving hundreds of clients worldwide. David's hands-on approach and emphasis on employee satisfaction ensured both the success of the business and the satisfaction of its clients. His expertise in digital marketing, business consulting, and strategic growth strategies has been honed through years of experience and a commitment to staying at the forefront of industry trends.

Released from prison in December 2020, David emerged with a renewed sense of purpose and a profound testimony of God's faithfulness. His journey serves as a testament to the enduring power of faith, the resilience of the human spirit, and the transformative grace of a God who offers second chances to all who seek Him. Today, David continues to share his story, inspiring others to embrace redemption, hope, and the boundless possibilities of a life surrendered to Christ.

Brand 316 Inc www.brand316.org 727 North Waco #290 Wichita KS 67203 (316) 247-2050

INTRODUCTION

Dear Brothers and Sisters in Christ,

Greetings in the name of our Lord and Savior, Jesus Christ! As we journey through life, it is crucial to remain focused on living a life devoted to Christ. As Christians, our relationship with Jesus Christ is the cornerstone of our faith and daily living. This relationship is not static but dynamic, requiring continual growth and deepening.

I was raised in a Christian household and attended church every week. Throughout my life, I read the Bible, but it was more out of obligation than genuine interest. I believed in God, but I never truly felt His presence. Everything changed for me when I was in prison, confined to an 8x10 cell. It was there that I developed a true desire to read and study the Bible. For the first time, I genuinely wanted to know God and understand His Word. It changed my life forever!

Studying the Bible is the foundation of Christian growth and spiritual maturity. It is through the diligent and consistent study of the Scriptures that we come to understand God's character, His will for our lives, and the truths that anchor our faith. The Bible is more than just a historical document or a collection of moral teachings; it is the living and active Word of God (Hebrews 4:12), a divine guide that lightens our path and shapes our worldview. Spending time in the Bible will change your life, it will give you hope for the future and help you better experience that we truly serve a God of second chances! I want to encourage you to use the Bible study as a platform to develop and grow your personal relationship with Christ. If you have never studied the Bible, this is a great tool for you. If you have studied the Bible for years, you will find this Bible study much different than others.

The Foundation of Faith

The Bible reveals who God is, His nature, and His plan for humanity. Through the pages of Scripture, we learn about God's love, justice, mercy, and sovereignty. The Bible tells the grand narrative of creation, fall, redemption, and restoration, centering on Jesus Christ as the fulfillment of God's redemptive plan.

Studying the Bible regularly allows us to build a solid foundation for our faith. Jesus Himself emphasized the importance of knowing the Scriptures. When tempted by Satan, Jesus responded with, "It is written," demonstrating His deep knowledge and reliance on God's Word (Matthew 4:4-10). Similarly, we are called to be rooted in Scripture, enabling us to stand firm against the challenges and temptations of life.

Spiritual Food and Growth

Just as food is necessary for our bodies, spiritual nourishment is essential for our souls. The Bible is often referred to as spiritual food – the bread of life (John 6:35) and milk for spiritual infants (1 Peter 2:2). Through regular Bible study, we are spiritually fed and strengthened. We grow in our understanding of God's promises, gain wisdom for daily living, and find encouragement in times of trouble.

Brand 316 Inc www.brand316.org 727 North Waco #290 Wichita KS 67203 (316) 247-2050

Paul's words to Timothy highlight the transformative power of Scripture: "All Scripture is God-breathed and is useful for teaching, rebuking, correcting and training in righteousness, so that the servant of God may be thoroughly equipped for every good work" (2 Timothy 3:16-17). Consistent studying of the Bible equips us for service, helps us discern right from wrong, and shapes us into the likeness of Christ.

Guidance and Wisdom

Life is full of decisions, challenges, and uncertainties. The Bible provides timeless wisdom and guidance for navigating life's difficulties. Psalm 119:105 declares, "Your word is a lamp for my feet, a light on my path." By immersing ourselves in Scripture, we gain clarity and direction, understanding God's will for our lives.

Biblical principles apply to all areas of life, from relationships and work to finances and personal conduct. They apply to you if you are in prison, recently released or have never had any interactions with the police. The stories of biblical characters and the teachings of Jesus and the apostles offer valuable lessons and insights. Through consistent study, we learn to apply these principles in practical ways, making decisions that honor God and reflect His wisdom. God has a long history of using our past failures for His glory – we will explore that in this Bible Study.

Strengthening Our Relationship with God

The Bible is not just a book to be read but a means to encounter God and deepen our relationship with Him. Through Scripture, God speaks to us, revealing His heart and inviting us into a closer walk with Him. The more we study the Bible, the more we come to know and love God.

In the Gospels, we see Jesus often withdrew to pray. He knew the Scriptures intimately and used them to teach, heal, and challenge. As His followers, we are called to do the same. Studying the Bible is a way to commune with God, to hear His voice, and to respond in obedience.

Defense Against False Teaching

In a world filled with diverse philosophies and beliefs, it is crucial to be grounded in the truth of God's Word. The Bible warns against false teachings and encourages believers to test everything against Scripture. Acts 17:11 commends the Bereans for their diligence in examining the Scriptures to verify Paul's teachings.

Staying in the Bible consistently helps us discern truth from error, protecting us from deception. It allows us to develop a biblical worldview, to think critically and biblically about the issues we face, and to stand firm in our faith amidst cultural pressures.

Building Community and Fellowship

Studying the Bible is not only an individual pursuit but also a group activity. Gathering with others to study Scripture creates fellowship, accountability, and mutual encouragement. In small groups or Bible study classes, we can discuss insights, ask questions, and share experiences, enriching our understanding of God's Word.

Hebrews 10:24-25 encourages believers to spur one another on toward love and good deeds and to not give up meeting together. Studying the Bible in community helps us grow together in faith, builds deeper relationships, and creates a supportive network of fellow believers. If you are able, you are encouraged to do this Bible study with others and specifically openly discuss the questions at the end of each lesson.

Transforming Our Lives

Ultimately, the goal is not merely to gain knowledge but to be transformed. James 1:22 urges us to be doers of the Word, not just hearers. As we study Scripture and apply its truths, our lives are changed. We become more like Christ, bearing the fruit of the Spirit and living out our faith in tangible ways.

The Bible calls us to love God with all our heart, soul, mind, and strength, and to love our neighbors as ourselves (Mark 12:30-31). By reading and understanding the Bible, we are empowered to live out these commands, to serve others, and to be a light in the world.

Pray and Read

It is important to prioritize studying the Bible and dedicating time and effort to immerse ourselves in Scripture. Before you open the book, spend one minute and pray to God for clarity and patience and that His words speak to you directly. Let us approach God's Word with humility, seeking to know Him more deeply and to be transformed by His truth.

With love and prayers,

David Phillips

David Phillips
Founder – Brand 316, Inc

If you are currently incarcerated, in a halfway house or in another type of facility please write us a letter upon completion of the workbook.

We will mail you an evaluation and assessment for you to complete. The assessment will include questions and answers in review to verify you completed the entire workbook along with a written impact statement.

Upon return and review, we will mail you the official certificate of completion and also a copy directly to your unit team so it can be placed in your file. If there are others (like a family member) you want the certificate mailed to please indicate that in your response to us.

Please Send Mail Directly To:

Brand 316, Inc
Attn: Completion Certificate - Forgiven and Free
727 North Waco Street
Suite 290
Wichita, KS 67203

Week 1: Imprisonment and Freedom: Prison and Prisoners in the Bible

Imprisonment is a recurring theme in the Bible, with numerous accounts of people who found themselves incarcerated for various reasons. From Joseph in Egypt to Paul in Rome, the Bible provides rich narratives of imprisonment and liberation, highlighting themes of justice, redemption, and divine intervention. In this lesson, we will look into the biblical teachings about prisoners, examining the experiences of notable figures who were imprisoned, and reflecting on the spiritual lessons we can glean from their stories.

Verse to Review: Hebrews 13:3

"Remember those in prison as if you were their fellow prisoners, and those who are mistreated as if you yourselves were suffering."

Imprisonment in the Bible:

Throughout the Bible, imprisonment is depicted as a consequence of wrongdoing, persecution, or injustice. There were also those imprisoned wrongfully or because of their love for Christ. However, prison is also portrayed as a place of divine encounter and transformation. Some of the key accounts of imprisonment in the Bible include:

1. **Joseph:** Joseph's story of imprisonment in Egypt is one of betrayal and resilience. Falsely accused by Potiphar's wife of attempted rape, Joseph found himself thrown into prison despite his innocence. Yet, even in the darkness of captivity, Joseph remained steadfast in his faith and integrity, interpreting dreams for fellow prisoners and ultimately gaining favor in the eyes of the prison warden. His time in prison was a test of character, preparing him for the eventual fulfillment of his dreams and his rise to prominence as a ruler in Egypt. **Genesis 39:20-23**

2. **Samson:** Samson, renowned for his extraordinary strength, fell victim to the schemes of Delilah, who betrayed him to the Philistines. Captured, blinded, and imprisoned by his enemies, Samson faced humiliation and suffering. However, even in his lowest moments, Samson's faith remained steadfast, and he prayed to God for strength one last time. In a final act of bravery, Samson brought down the temple of Dagon upon himself and his captors, demonstrating his unwavering commitment to God's will and the deliverance of his people from oppression. **Judges 16:21-25**

3. **Jeremiah:** As a prophet called to deliver messages of judgment and repentance to the people of Judah, Jeremiah faced opposition and persecution from those who rejected his words. Imprisoned multiple times for his outspokenness, Jeremiah endured hardship and suffering for the sake of his divine calling. Yet, even in captivity, Jeremiah remained faithful to his mission, continuing to proclaim God's truth to all who would listen, despite the personal cost. **Jeremiah 37:11-16, Jeremiah 38:6-13**

Brand 316 Inc www.brand316.org 727 North Waco #290 Wichita KS 67203 (316) 247-2050

4. **John the Baptist:** John the Baptist's imprisonment by King Herod Antipas was a consequence of his bold condemnation of Herod's unlawful marriage to Herodias, his brother's wife. Despite being unjustly imprisoned for speaking out against sin, John continued to uphold the principles of righteousness and prepare the way for the coming of the Messiah. His imprisonment ultimately led to his martyrdom, as Herodias's daughter requested his head on a platter, fulfilling Herod's rash oath. **Matthew 14:3-12, Mark 6:17-29**

5. **Paul:** Paul's imprisonment was a testament to his unwavering commitment to spreading the gospel despite the opposition he faced. Whether in Philippi, Caesarea, or Rome, Paul used his time in captivity to preach the message of salvation, even converting some of his jailers and fellow prisoners. His letters written from prison, including Ephesians, Philippians, Colossians, and Philemon, continue to inspire and instruct believers today, demonstrating the power of faith in the midst of adversity. **Acts 16:16-40 (Philippi), Acts 23:23-35 (Caesarea), Acts 28:16, 30-31 (Rome)**

6. **Peter:** Peter's miraculous escape from prison serves as a powerful example of God's intervention on behalf of his faithful servants. Despite being imprisoned by King Herod Agrippa I and facing imminent execution, Peter remained steadfast in prayer, trusting in God's deliverance. An angel of the Lord appeared to him, supernaturally releasing him from his chains and leading him out of the prison, illustrating the divine protection afforded to those who remain faithful to God's purposes. **Acts 12:1-19**

7. **Silas:** Silas, a companion of Paul on his missionary journeys, shared in his imprisonment in Philippi. Despite the injustice of their confinement, Silas and Paul used their time in prison to worship and pray, resulting in a miraculous deliverance orchestrated by God. Their steadfast faith and praise in the midst of adversity not only led to their physical liberation but also served as a powerful testimony to the watching world of God's faithfulness and power. **Acts 16:16-40 (Philippi)**

8. **Micaiah:** Micaiah's imprisonment by King Ahab of Israel exemplifies the persecution faced by prophets who dared to speak God's truth to corrupt rulers. Despite being imprisoned for his prophetic warnings against Ahab's wickedness, Micaiah remained resolute in his commitment to proclaiming God's word. His imprisonment serves as a reminder of the cost of speaking truth to power and the faithfulness required to stand firm in the face of opposition. **1 Kings 22:26-27**

9. **Hanani:** Hanani, a prophet who confronted King Asa of Judah for relying on foreign alliances instead of trusting in God, was imprisoned as a result of his bold rebuke. Despite the personal risk involved, Hanani remained faithful to his prophetic calling, challenging the king to repentance and obedience. His imprisonment highlights the courage required to speak truth to authority, even at great personal cost, and the importance of remaining faithful to God's commands regardless of the consequences. **2 Chronicles 16:7-10**

Biblical Teachings about Prisoners:

The Bible provides comprehensive teachings guiding believers on how to engage with prisoners and those who are oppressed, emphasizing empathy, ministry, justice, mercy, forgiveness, and restoration. Some of these teachings include:

- **Compassion and Empathy:** Scripture urges believers to remember and empathize with those who are imprisoned, recognizing their inherent dignity as fellow human beings created in the image of God (Hebrews 13:3). This call to compassion encourages believers to extend love and care to prisoners, acknowledging their humanity and worth despite their circumstances.

- **Ministry of Reconciliation:** Jesus Himself highlighted the importance of ministering to prisoners, stating that visiting those in prison is a tangible expression of our commitment to the gospel of reconciliation and redemption (Matthew 25:36). Engaging in prison ministry provides an opportunity for believers to share the transformative message of Christ's love and forgiveness, offering hope and healing to those who are incarcerated.

- **Justice and Mercy:** The Bible underscores the significance of seeking justice for the oppressed and marginalized, advocating for fair treatment and rehabilitation of prisoners (Micah 6:8). This mandate involves addressing systemic injustices within the criminal justice system and promoting policies and practices that uphold human dignity and promote restoration. Additionally, the biblical principle of mercy calls believers to extend compassion and support to those who have made mistakes or fallen into sin, recognizing the potential for redemption and transformation.

- **Forgiveness and Restoration:** As recipients of God's grace and forgiveness, believers are called to extend the same forgiveness and offer hope to prisoners (Colossians 3:13). Embracing a spirit of forgiveness enables people to break the cycle of bitterness and resentment, fostering an environment conducive to healing and restoration. By extending grace and compassion, believers can play a pivotal role in facilitating the process of rehabilitation and reconciliation for those who are incarcerated.

The biblical teachings on engaging with prisoners and the oppressed emphasize the importance of compassion, ministry, justice, mercy, forgiveness, and restoration.

Conclusion:

The biblical narratives of imprisonment and liberation serve as profound testaments to God's sovereignty and providence amidst the trials of human suffering and injustice. These stories intricately weave together themes of resilience, faithfulness, and divine intervention, portraying people who, even amid the darkest depths of their trials, remained unwavering in their trust in God. Through their unwavering faith, they exemplify the enduring hope and assurance found in God's promises. As believers, we are called to emulate their steadfast example, extending not only compassion, mercy, and hope but also actively advocating for justice and righteousness in a world marked by brokenness and oppression.

Furthermore, the teachings of Christ challenge us to reassess our attitudes and assumptions regarding prisoners and the marginalized in society. Jesus, in identifying Himself with the least of society, profoundly declared that acts of kindness and compassion toward the marginalized are, in fact, direct expressions of love and service to Him (Matthew 25:40). This transformative perspective compels us to engage in acts of mercy, including ministering to prisoners, visiting the sick, and standing in solidarity with the oppressed. By embracing this holistic approach to ministry, we embody the essence of the gospel, which champions reconciliation, restoration, and liberation for all.

Moreover, the biblical teachings about prisoners underscore the transformative power of forgiveness and reconciliation. Central to the gospel message is the profound truth that every individual, regardless of their past mistakes or failures, is a recipient of God's boundless grace and unconditional love. Through the redemptive work of Christ, prisoners find liberation from the shackles of sin and brokenness, experiencing profound healing and restoration. As believers, we are commissioned to extend the same forgiveness and hope we have received to those who are incarcerated, serving as ambassadors of reconciliation and agents of God's transformative grace.

Imprisonment and liberation are recurring themes in the Bible, reflecting the complexities of human nature and the divine intervention of God in the lives of His people. The Bible offers rich narratives and profound teachings about imprisonment and liberation, compelling us to examine our own attitudes and actions toward prisoners. As we immerse ourselves in these timeless truths, may we be inspired to emulate the example of Christ by extending compassion, mercy, and hope to all who are in need.

Reflective Questions - Answer in Writing

1. How do the biblical accounts of imprisonment challenge your understanding of justice and mercy?

2. In what ways can you show compassion and empathy towards prisoners and those who are oppressed in your community?

3. Reflect on a time when you experienced God's liberation from spiritual bondage or captivity. How has this impacted your perspective on imprisonment and redemption?

4. Consider the role of forgiveness and reconciliation in ministering to prisoners. How can you extend grace and offer hope to those who are incarcerated?

5. How does the biblical teaching about prisoners challenge you to engage in advocacy and social justice initiatives in your community?

Week 2: 1 Corinthians 13:11 - Growing in Spiritual Maturity

1 Corinthians 13:11 reflects on the journey from childhood to maturity, illustrating the importance of growing in understanding and love as believers. This verse is part of the famous "Love Chapter," which emphasizes the supremacy of love in the Christian life.

The Book of 1 Corinthians

1 Corinthians is an epistle written by the Apostle Paul to the church in Corinth. The letter addresses various issues within the church, including divisions, immorality, and misunderstandings about spiritual gifts. Paul emphasizes the need for unity, purity, and love among believers.

Immediate Context

1 Corinthians 13, often referred to as the "Love Chapter," is a profound exposition on the nature and importance of love. Paul discusses the qualities of love and its superiority over spiritual gifts. Verse 11 specifically addresses the concept of maturity in the context of love, using the metaphor of growing from childhood to adulthood.

Exploring 1 Corinthians 13:11

The Text

"When I was a child, I talked like a child, I thought like a child, I reasoned like a child. When I became a man, I put the ways of childhood behind me." (1 Corinthians 13:11, NIV)

Key Phrases

1. **"When I was a child, I talked like a child, I thought like a child, I reasoned like a child"**

    o   This phrase highlights the natural characteristics of childhood—innocence, simplicity, and limited understanding.

2. **"When I became a man, I put the ways of childhood behind me"**

    o   This indicates a transition to maturity, where childish ways are abandoned in favor of mature thinking, reasoning, and behavior.

Theological Implications

Spiritual Maturity

Paul uses the metaphor of growing from childhood to adulthood to illustrate the call to spiritual maturity. Just as physical and intellectual growth is expected in human development, spiritual growth is

Brand 316 Inc www.brand316.org 727 North Waco #290 Wichita KS 67203 (316) 247-2050

expected in the Christian life. We grow spiritually through immersing ourselves in the Bible, worshipping, fellowship and praying.

The Role of Love in Maturity

The entire chapter emphasizes that love is the mark of true maturity. Spiritual gifts and knowledge, while important, are incomplete without love. Maturing in faith means growing in love, reflecting Christ's love in our actions and relationships.

Putting Away Childish Ways

This involves moving beyond immature behaviors, thoughts, and attitudes. It means embracing a deeper, more sacrificial love that seeks the well-being of others over personal gain.

Practical Applications

Embracing Spiritual Growth

- **Commit to Learning**: Regularly study the Bible and seek to understand its teachings deeply. Participate in Bible studies, read theological books, and engage in discussions to grow in knowledge and wisdom. Pray for guidance and understanding as well.

- **Seek Godly Mentors**: Find mature Christians who can guide and support you in your spiritual journey. Learn from their experiences and insights.

Practicing Mature Love

- **Act with Compassion**: Demonstrate love through acts of kindness, service, and compassion. Look for opportunities to help others and show God's love in practical ways.

- **Grow in Patience and Understanding**: Practice patience and understanding in your relationships. Listen actively, forgive readily, and seek to resolve conflicts with grace.

Reflecting on Personal Growth

- **Self-Examination**: Regularly examine your thoughts, words, and actions. Identify areas where you may still be acting in childish ways and commit to growth in those areas.

- **Prayer for Transformation**: Pray for God's help in transforming your heart and mind. Ask Him to help you grow in love, wisdom, and maturity.

Misunderstandings and Cautions

Misinterpreting Childhood as Negative

Brand 316 Inc www.brand316.org 727 North Waco #290 Wichita KS 67203 (316) 247-2050

Paul's reference to childhood is not meant to demean childlike qualities such as innocence or dependence on God. Rather, it highlights the need for growth and maturity in understanding and love.

Neglecting the Importance of Love

In the pursuit of spiritual growth, it's essential not to overlook the importance of love. Knowledge, spiritual gifts, and achievements are meaningless without love. Ensure that your growth is marked by an increasing capacity to love others selflessly.

Biblical Examples

Jesus' Growth in Wisdom and Stature

In Luke 2:52, it is said that Jesus grew in wisdom and stature and in favor with God and man. Jesus' development from childhood to adulthood exemplifies balanced growth in physical, intellectual, and spiritual areas. His life is a model of maturity and love.

The Apostle Peter

Peter's journey from impulsive fisherman to a mature leader in the early church illustrates significant spiritual growth. Initially characterized by impulsiveness and misunderstanding, Peter grew to become a wise and loving shepherd of God's people, as seen in Acts and his epistles.

The Corinthian Church

The recipients of Paul's letter, the Corinthians, struggled with divisions, immorality, and immature behavior. Paul's exhortation to grow in love and maturity was a direct response to their need for spiritual development and unity.

Conclusion

1 Corinthians 13:11 challenges believers to grow from spiritual childhood to maturity, marked by love and wisdom. We are called to mature in our faith and relationships. This means we need to leave behind childish ways and grow in love, reflecting Christ in our actions and interactions. Let us commit to this journey of growth, seeking to embody the mature, selfless love that Paul describes. By doing so, we honor God and build up His church in unity and strength.

Reflective Questions – Answer in Writing

1. How can you actively pursue spiritual growth and maturity in your daily life?

2. In what areas of your life do you need to put away childish ways and embrace mature thinking and behavior? We all have them, list them out and create a plan!

3. How can you demonstrate mature love in your relationships and interactions with others?

4. What practical steps can you take to be more patient in your life?

5. What are small acts of kindness that you can do for others to show God's Love?

Week 3: Psalm 68:5-6 - God's Provision for the Lonely and Vulnerable

Psalm 68:5-6 is a beautiful passage that highlights God's care and provision for the vulnerable and marginalized in society. It speaks of God's compassion for the fatherless, widows, and the lonely, emphasizing His desire to provide a home and freedom. This study will explore the context, meaning, and application of Psalm 68:5-6, helping us understand how it reflects God's heart for the oppressed and His call for us to do the same.

The Book of Psalms

The Book of Psalms is a collection of songs, prayers, and poems that express a wide range of emotions and experiences, from deep despair to enthusiastic praise. Many of the Psalms were written by King David, while others were created by different authors.

Immediate Context

Psalm 68 is a song of triumph and celebration, attributed to David. It praises God for His power, majesty, and victorious acts. The psalm recounts God's past deliverances, His care for His people, and His righteous judgment against His enemies. Verses 5-6 specifically highlight God's compassionate character and His care for the vulnerable.

Exploring Psalm 68:5-6

The Text

"A father to the fatherless, a defender of widows, is God in his holy dwelling. God sets the lonely in families, he leads out the prisoners with singing; but the rebellious live in a sun-scorched land" (Psalm 68:5-6, NIV).

Key Phrases

1. **"A father to the fatherless, a defender of widows"**

   o   This phrase emphasizes God's special concern for those who are most vulnerable in society, providing them with protection and care. This includes you!

2. **"Is God in his holy dwelling"**

   o   It highlights that God's compassion and justice come from His holy nature and His divine presence.

3. **"God sets the lonely in families"**

- o This phrase illustrates God's desire to provide community and belonging for those who are isolated or lonely.

4. **"He leads out the prisoners with singing"**

   - o It signifies God's power to bring freedom and joy to those who are oppressed or imprisoned. Praise the Lord!

5. **"But the rebellious live in a sun-scorched land"**

   - o This serves as a warning that those who resist God's ways will face desolation and hardship.

Theological Implications

God's Compassion and Justice

Psalm 68:5-6 reveals God's deep compassion for the marginalized and His commitment to justice. He identifies Himself as a protector and provider for the fatherless and widows, demonstrating His care for the most vulnerable.

Divine Provision

God's provision is seen in His act of placing the lonely in families and leading prisoners to freedom. This illustrates His desire to restore and uplift those who are suffering or marginalized.

Righteous Judgment

The verse also includes a warning that rebellion against God leads to desolation. It underscores the importance of aligning with God's ways to experience His blessings.

Practical Applications

Caring for the Vulnerable

As believers, we are called to emulate God's compassion by caring for the fatherless, widows, and others who are vulnerable. This can involve providing support, protection, and community for those in need.

Building Community

We can follow God's example by creating inclusive and welcoming communities that provide a sense of belonging for the lonely. This might involve reaching out to those who are isolated and inviting them into our circles.

Advocating for Justice

God's commitment to justice should inspire us to advocate for the oppressed and marginalized in society. This can involve supporting policies and initiatives that protect and uplift those who are vulnerable. Justice is a common theme throughout the Bible.

Misunderstandings and Cautions

Misinterpreting God's Compassion

While God's compassion is boundless, it is also coupled with His justice. This means that while we are called to care for the vulnerable, we must also uphold principles of justice and righteousness.

Overlooking the Call to Action

It's important not to overlook the call to action in these verses. God's compassion should move us to actively engage in caring for the helpless, rather than simply feeling sympathetic.

Balancing Compassion and Justice

We must balance our acts of compassion with a commitment to justice, ensuring that our efforts to help the vulnerable are done in a way that promotes fairness and righteousness.

Biblical Examples

Ruth and Naomi

The story of Ruth and Naomi (Ruth 1-4) exemplifies God's care for widows. Naomi, a widow, experiences God's provision through her daughter-in-law Ruth, who remains loyal and eventually marries Boaz. Boaz acts as a kinsman-redeemer, reflecting God's provision and protection for vulnerable individuals.

Elijah and the Widow of Zarephath

In 1 Kings 17:8-24, Elijah encounters a widow during a time of severe famine. Despite her own desperate circumstances, the widow obeys Elijah's request to prepare a meal for him. God miraculously provides for the widow and her son, demonstrating His care for those who are vulnerable and obedient.

Conclusion

Psalm 68:5-6 beautifully highlights God's compassionate nature and His commitment to caring for the vulnerable. By understanding its context, meaning, and practical applications, we can be inspired to reflect God's character in our own lives.

As Christians, we are called to mimic God's compassion and justice by caring for the fatherless, widows, and other vulnerable people. Let us build inclusive communities, advocate for justice, and actively engage in acts of compassion, trusting in God's promise to provide and protect. By doing so, we reflect God's heart and bring His love and justice to a hurting world.

Reflective Questions - Answer in Writing

1. Read Psalm 68:5-6 again. What part of the verse stands out to you the most and why?

2. When have you experienced God's provision and protection in your own life?

3. How can you actively respond to God's call to extend compassion and care to those in need where you are now?

4. Reflect on the imagery of God setting the lonely in families and leading prisoners to freedom. In what ways can you participate in God's work of bringing healing and restoration to those who are hurting?

5. How does it inspire you to advocate for justice, build community, and pray for deliverance for the lonely and vulnerable in your midst?

Week 4: The Prodigal Son - Redemption and Unconditional Love

Luke 15:11-32, also known as the Parable of the Prodigal Son, is one of Jesus' most well-known parables. This story illustrates the themes of repentance, forgiveness, and the boundless grace and love of God. This parable explains in a clear and easy to understand way God's heart for the lost and His readiness to forgive.

The Gospel of Luke

The Gospel of Luke is known for its emphasis on Jesus' compassion and outreach to the marginalized. Luke meticulously recounts Jesus' parables, teachings, and miracles, providing a comprehensive picture of His ministry and mission.

Immediate Context

Luke 15 contains three parables about lost things: the lost sheep, the lost coin, and the lost son. These parables are Jesus' response to the Pharisees and scribes who criticized Him for associating with sinners. The Parable of the Prodigal Son, the most detailed of the three, illustrates God's joy over a sinner's repentance.

Exploring Luke 15:11-32

The Text

"Jesus continued: 'There was a man who had two sons. The younger one said to his father, "Father, give me my share of the estate." So he divided his property between them. Not long after that, the younger son got together all he had, set off for a distant country and there squandered his wealth in wild living. After he had spent everything, there was a severe famine in that whole country, and he began to be in need. So he went and hired himself out to a citizen of that country, who sent him to his fields to feed pigs. He longed to fill his stomach with the pods that the pigs were eating, but no one gave him anything.'

'When he came to his senses, he said, "How many of my father's hired servants have food to spare, and here I am starving to death! I will set out and go back to my father and say to him: Father, I have sinned against heaven and against you. I am no longer worthy to be called your son; make me like one of your hired servants." So he got up and went to his father.'

'But while he was still a long way off, his father saw him and was filled with compassion for him; he ran to his son, threw his arms around him and kissed him. The son said to him, "Father, I have sinned against heaven and against you. I am no longer worthy to be called your son." But the father said to his servants, "Quick! Bring the best robe and put it on him. Put a ring on his finger and sandals on his feet.

Bring the fattened calf and kill it. Let's have a feast and celebrate. For this son of mine was dead and is alive again; he was lost and is found." So they began to celebrate.'

'Meanwhile, the older son was in the field. When he came near the house, he heard music and dancing. So he called one of the servants and asked him what was going on. "Your brother has come," he replied, "and your father has killed the fattened calf because he has him back safe and sound." The older brother became angry and refused to go in. So his father went out and pleaded with him. But he answered his father, "Look! All these years I've been slaving for you and never disobeyed your orders. Yet you never gave me even a young goat so I could celebrate with my friends. But when this son of yours who has squandered your property with prostitutes comes home, you kill the fattened calf for him!"'

'"My son," the father said, "you are always with me, and everything I have is yours. But we had to celebrate and be glad, because this brother of yours was dead and is alive again; he was lost and is found."'" (Luke 15:11-32, NIV)

Key Phrases

1. **"Father, give me my share of the estate."**

   o The younger son's demand for his inheritance reflects a desire for independence and a disregard for his father's authority and provision. This was also an insult to the father essentially acting as if the father was dead to him.

2. **"He squandered his wealth in wild living."**

   o This phrase highlights the reckless and irresponsible behavior of the younger son, leading to his downfall.

3. **"When he came to his senses."**

   o This turning point signifies the son's realization of his mistakes and his decision to return to his father, symbolizing repentance.

4. **"His father saw him and was filled with compassion."**

   o The father's immediate compassion and action upon seeing his son reflects God's readiness to forgive and welcome back those who repent.

5. **"The older brother became angry."**

   o The older brother's reaction represents the self-righteousness and lack of compassion that can hinder true forgiveness and reconciliation.

Theological Implications

The Nature of Sin and Repentance

The younger son's journey illustrates the destructive nature of sin and the importance of repentance. His reckless actions lead to dire consequences, but his recognition of his wrongdoing and return to his father symbolizes true repentance.

The Father's Forgiveness

The father's response to his returning son represents God's boundless grace and forgiveness. He does not wait for the son to arrive but runs to meet him, showing that God eagerly awaits and embraces those who turn back to Him.

The Danger of Self-Righteousness

The older brother's attitude highlights the danger of self-righteousness and a lack of forgiveness. His inability to rejoice in his brother's return reveals a heart hardened by pride, anger and resentment.

Practical Applications

Embracing Repentance

Recognize the importance of repentance in your spiritual journey. Like the younger son, come to your senses, acknowledge your sins, and return to God with a humble and contrite heart.

Reflecting God's Grace

Mimic the father's example by extending grace and forgiveness to others. Be quick to forgive and ready to reconcile, showing the same compassion that God has shown you.

Avoiding Self-Righteousness

Guard against self-righteous attitudes that can hinder your ability to forgive and rejoice in others' redemption. Cultivate a heart of humility and empathy, celebrating the restoration of those who repent.

Misunderstandings and Cautions

Misinterpreting God's Forgiveness

Some may misunderstand God's forgiveness as a license to sin. Understand that true repentance involves a sincere turning away from sin and a commitment to living according to God's will.

Overlooking the Need for Repentance

While God's grace is abundant, it requires a response of repentance. Emphasize the importance of acknowledging and turning away from sin to experience the fullness of God's forgiveness.

Ignoring the Older Brother's Lesson

The parable is not just about the prodigal son but also about the older brother. Reflect on the older brother's attitude and your own tendencies towards self-righteousness and lack of compassion.

Biblical Examples

The Prodigal Son

The younger son's journey from rebellion to repentance illustrates the transformative power of recognizing one's sin and returning to God. His story encourages us to seek forgiveness and trust in God's mercy.

Jonah

In the Book of Jonah, the prophet initially runs away from God's command to preach to Nineveh. After a series of events, he repents and fulfills his mission, demonstrating God's willingness to use even those who initially rebel against Him.

The Apostle Paul

Paul, formerly Saul, persecuted Christians before encountering Jesus on the road to Damascus. His radical transformation and subsequent ministry exemplify the power of God's grace and forgiveness in a repentant heart.

Conclusion

Luke 15:11-32, the Parable of the Prodigal Son, offers profound insights into the themes of repentance, forgiveness, and God's boundless grace. It is pivotal to recognize our need for repentance, reflect God's grace in our interactions with others, and guard against self-righteous attitudes. Let us commit to living out these principles, extending compassion and forgiveness, and celebrating the redemption of those who return to God. By doing so, we mirror the heart of our Heavenly Father and participate in His work of restoration and reconciliation.

Reflective Questions - Answer in Writing

1. How does the story of the prodigal son make you think about repentance and forgiveness?

2. In what ways can you extend grace and compassion to those who have wronged you, following the example of the father in the parable?

3. Reflect on a time when you experienced God's forgiveness. How can this experience shape your interactions with others?

4. Are there people in your life you need to forgive or ask for forgiveness? If so, what would be the smartest way to approach that?

5. What steps can you take to celebrate and support the restoration of those who repent and return to God?

Week 5: Smart and Godly Choices - Justifying Your Options Using the Bible

The Bible, as the divinely inspired Word of God, serves as a foundational guide for Christians in making decisions that align with God's will. It provides wisdom, principles, and examples to help believers navigate life's challenges and choices. **However, it's crucial to approach Scripture with a humble and open heart, seeking God's guidance rather than merely seeking validation for pre-determined decisions.** This study explores how Christians can align their choices with biblical principles while avoiding the pitfall of using Scripture to justify personal desires.

Aligning Decisions with Biblical Principles

Understanding God's Will

One of the fundamental ways Christians can align their decisions with the Bible is by seeking to understand God's will. Romans 12:2 (NIV) states, "Do not conform to the pattern of this world, but be transformed by the renewing of your mind. Then you will be able to test and approve what God's will is—his good, pleasing and perfect will." This verse emphasizes the importance of renewing our minds through Scripture to discern God's will. You can take active steps to follow advice through prayer, worship, having Christian mentors and constantly reading the Bible.

To understand God's will, Christians should:

- **Pray for Guidance**: James 1:5 (NIV) encourages believers to ask for wisdom: "If any of you lacks wisdom, you should ask God, who gives generously to all without finding fault, and it will be given to you." Prayer is pivotal for your long term decision making process.
- **Study the Bible**: Regular and systematic study of the Bible helps believers understand God's character, commands, and desires for their lives. The more you are in the Word, the closer you are to God.
- **Seek Counsel**: Proverbs 15:22 (NIV) states, "Plans fail for lack of counsel, but with many advisers they succeed." Seeking advice from mature Christians can provide clarity and confirmation. Focus on Christians that have been faithful for years, live a stable and Godly life and have proven themselves as people that follow the Word of God in all aspects of their life.

Applying Biblical Principles

The Bible offers numerous principles that can guide decision-making. Please take time to read each one and think about a specific future or past scenario where you either used that principle or should have :

- **Love and Compassion**: Jesus emphasized love as the greatest commandment (Matthew 22:37-40). Decisions should reflect love for God and others.
- **Integrity and Honesty**: Proverbs 10:9 (NIV) states, "Whoever walks in integrity walks securely, but whoever takes crooked paths will be found out."
- **Justice and Mercy**: Micah 6:8 (NIV) highlights the importance of acting justly and loving mercy.

29

- **Humility and Service**: Philippians 2:3-4 (NIV) urges believers to "do nothing out of selfish ambition or vain conceit. Rather, in humility value others above yourselves, not looking to your own interests but each of you to the interests of the others."

The Danger of Eisegesis: Reading into Scripture

Definition and Examples – What is Eisegesis? (Pronounce it: ek·suh·jee·suhs

Eisegesis is the process of interpreting a text by reading into it one's own ideas, biases, or desires, rather than drawing out its intended meaning. This practice can lead to misinterpretation and misuse of Scripture.

Examples of eisegesis include:

- **Selective Reading**: Choosing verses that support a predetermined decision while ignoring others that might offer a different perspective.
- **Context Ignorance**: Taking verses out of their historical, cultural, or literary context to make them fit a specific situation.
- **Personal Bias**: Allowing personal desires, fears, or preferences to shape the interpretation of Scripture.

Cautionary Advice

To avoid the pitfalls of eisegesis, Christians should approach the Bible with humility and a desire to understand God's truth:

- **Seek the Whole Counsel of God**: Acts 20:27 (NIV) speaks of declaring the whole counsel of God. It's essential to consider the entirety of Scripture rather than isolating individual verses.
- **Understand Context**: Studying the historical, cultural, and literary context of a passage can help uncover its true meaning.
- **Use Reliable Resources**: Commentaries, study Bibles, and other scholarly resources can provide valuable insights into the original meaning of the text.
- **Be Willing to Be Challenged**: Allow Scripture to challenge and change your preconceived notions and decisions.
- **Most Importantly Pray and stay in the Word**: The more you stay in the Bible, the closer you are to God and understanding His desires for you.

Case Examples: Justifying Choices with the Bible

Case Study 1: Financial Decisions

Scenario: A Christian businessman wants to justify a risky investment with the potential for high returns.

Biblical Principles:

- **Stewardship**: The Bible teaches that we are stewards of God's resources (Matthew 25:14-30).

- **Wisdom**: Proverbs 21:5 (NIV) says, "The plans of the diligent lead to profit as surely as haste leads to poverty."

Eisegesis Danger: The businessman might selectively use verses about God's blessings (e.g., Deuteronomy 8:18) to justify a potentially reckless decision, ignoring verses that warn against greed and the love of money (1 Timothy 6:10).

Proper Approach: He should seek God's wisdom through prayer, study the principles of stewardship and diligence in Scripture, and consult with trusted Christian advisors to ensure his decision aligns with biblical principles.

Case Study 2: Relationships

Scenario: A Christian woman wants to justify entering a romantic relationship with a non-believer.

Biblical Principles:

- **Spiritual Unity**: 2 Corinthians 6:14 (NIV) advises, "Do not be yoked together with unbelievers."
- **Love and Witness**: Christians are called to love others and be witnesses of Christ's love (John 13:34-35).

Eisegesis Danger: She might focus on verses that emphasize love and evangelism to justify the relationship, while neglecting the broader biblical teaching on spiritual unity in marriage.

Proper Approach: She should consider the full counsel of Scripture regarding relationships and seek advice from mature believers. Prayerfully discerning God's will and prioritizing spiritual unity will guide her to a decision that honors God.

Case Study 3: Ethical Dilemmas

Scenario: A Christian employee is asked to engage in questionable practices at work.

Biblical Principles:

- **Integrity**: Proverbs 11:3 (NIV) states, "The integrity of the upright guides them, but the unfaithful are destroyed by their duplicity."
- **Obedience to God**: Acts 5:29 (NIV) says, "We must obey God rather than human beings."

Eisegesis Danger: The employee might rationalize their actions by focusing on verses about obeying authorities (Romans 13:1), while ignoring those that emphasize integrity and obedience to God's commands.

Proper Approach: The employee should consider the broader biblical context of integrity and obedience to God. Seeking God's guidance through prayer, studying relevant Scripture passages, and consulting with trusted Christian mentors will help them make a decision that aligns with their faith.

Practical Steps for Making Biblically-Aligned Decisions

1. **Pray for Guidance**: Begin with prayer, asking God for wisdom and discernment in your decision-making process (James 1:5).
2. **Study the Bible Systematically**: Regularly read and study the Bible to understand God's principles and commands. Use study tools and resources to gain deeper insights.
3. **Seek Wise Counsel**: Consult with mature Christians, pastors, or spiritual mentors who can provide godly advice and perspective (Proverbs 15:22).
4. **Evaluate Your Motives**: Reflect on your motives and desires, ensuring they align with God's will and purposes. Ask yourself if your decision honors God and reflects His character.
5. **Consider the Impact**: Think about the potential consequences of your decision on yourself, others, and your witness for Christ. Ensure your actions promote love, justice, and mercy.
6. **Be Open to Correction**: Be willing to adjust your plans if God's Word or wise counsel indicates you are heading in the wrong direction.

Conclusion

Making decisions that align with biblical principles requires a heart attuned to God's will, a mind transformed by His Word, and a spirit open to His guidance. By approaching Scripture with humility, seeking the whole counsel of God, and avoiding the pitfalls of eisegesis, Christians can navigate life's choices in a manner that honors God and reflects His character. Let us commit to grounding our decisions in the truth of God's Word, always seeking to align our lives with His perfect will, and extending compassion, mercy, and love to those around us.

Reflective Questions - Answer in Writing

1. What are the key steps a Christian should take to ensure their decisions align with biblical principles?

2. Why is it important to avoid eisegesis when making decisions?

3. How can Christians balance the need for personal guidance from Scripture with the broader context of biblical teachings?

4. What are some practical ways to evaluate whether your motives and desires align with God's will when making a decision?

5. Based on the case studies provided, how can Christians apply biblical principles to specific situations such as financial decisions, relationships, and ethical dilemmas at work?

Week 6: Joshua 1:9 - Courage and Strength in God's Promises

Joshua 1:9 is a powerful verse that encourages believers to be strong and courageous, trusting in God's presence and support. It is important to know and understand no matter where you are or your situation you are in, God is with you. Let's explore Joshua 1:9.

The Book of Joshua

The Book of Joshua follows the first five books of the Bible, known as the Pentateuch. It details the leadership of Joshua, the successor to Moses, and the Israelites' conquest and settlement of the Promised Land. The book emphasizes God's faithfulness, the importance of obedience, and the fulfillment of God's promises to Israel.

Immediate Context

Joshua 1 begins with God speaking to Joshua after the death of Moses. God commissions Joshua to lead the Israelites into the Promised Land, assuring him of His presence and support. Verses 6-9 are particularly focused on encouraging Joshua to be strong and courageous, emphasizing the need for faithfulness to God's law and the assurance of God's presence.

Exploring Joshua 1:9

The Text

"Have I not commanded you? Be strong and courageous. Do not be afraid; do not be discouraged, for the Lord your God will be with you wherever you go" (Joshua 1:9, NIV).

Key Phrases

1. **"Have I not commanded you?"**

   o   This phrase emphasizes that the command to be strong and courageous comes directly from God, giving it great authority and importance.

2. **"Be strong and courageous."**

   o   This is both a command and an encouragement. Strength and courage are essential qualities for facing challenges and fulfilling God's purposes.

3. **"Do not be afraid; do not be discouraged."**

   o   Fear and discouragement are natural human responses to tough situations, but God instructs Joshua to overcome these feelings by trusting in Him. We should do the same.

Brand 316 Inc www.brand316.org 727 North Waco #290 Wichita KS 67203 (316) 247-2050

4. **"For the Lord your God will be with you wherever you go."**

   o   The promise of God's continual presence is the basis for Joshua's strength and courage. God's presence assures Joshua of guidance, protection, and support.

Theological Implications

Divine Command

Joshua 1:9 underscores that strength and courage are not merely personal virtues but are commanded by God. This command is rooted in God's authority and His plan for His people.

Trust in God's Presence

The verse highlights the importance of trusting in God's presence. Knowing that God is with us can dispel fear and discouragement, empowering us to face challenges with confidence.

Obedience and Faithfulness

Joshua's strength and courage are linked to his obedience to God's commands. Faithfulness to God's Word is essential for experiencing His guidance and support.

Practical Applications

Facing Challenges with Courage

In our lives, we face various challenges that can evoke fear and discouragement. Joshua 1:9 encourages us to be strong and courageous, trusting that God is with us in every situation.

Trusting God's Promises

We can find assurance in God's promises, knowing that He is faithful. His presence and support are guaranteed, just as they were for Joshua, enabling us to move forward with confidence.

Overcoming Fear and Discouragement

When we feel afraid or discouraged, we can remember Joshua 1:9 and draw strength from God's command and promise. Prayer, meditation on Scripture, and seeking God's guidance can help us overcome negative emotions and tough situations.

Misunderstandings and Cautions

Misinterpreting Courage

Courage does not mean recklessness or ignoring risks. It involves trusting God while wisely assessing and responding to situations. Strength and courage should be balanced with caution and discernment.

Assuming Immediate Results

God's presence does not guarantee immediate success or the absence of difficulties. It means we have His support and guidance through the process, regardless of the outcome.

Overlooking the Need for Obedience

The promise of God's presence is tied to obedience. Ignoring God's commands can lead to unnecessary difficulties. Faithful living is crucial for experiencing the fullness of God's support.

Biblical Examples

Joshua's Leadership

Joshua's leadership in the conquest of Canaan exemplifies the application of Joshua 1:9. Despite numerous challenges, including battles and resistance, Joshua remained strong and courageous, trusting in God's presence and leading the Israelites to victory.

Modern-Day Application

Consider a modern Christian facing a major life decision or challenge, such as prison, a career change, a health issue, or a personal crisis. By applying the principles of Joshua 1:9, they can find strength and courage, knowing that God is with them and will guide them through the situation.

Conclusion

Joshua 1:9 is a powerful and encouraging verse that calls us to be strong and courageous, trusting in God's presence and support. By understanding its context, meaning, and practical relevance, we can draw strength from this verse and apply its principles to our lives.

As Christians, we are called to face challenges with courage and trust in God's promises. Let us embrace the command to be strong and courageous, overcoming fear and discouragement by relying on God's continual presence no matter the situation we are in now. By doing so, we can confidently pursue God's purposes for our lives, knowing that He is with us wherever we go.

Reflective Questions - Answer in Writing

1. How does Joshua 1:9 challenge your understanding of courage and strength in the Christian life?

2. Reflect on a time when you experienced God's presence and provision in the midst of challenges. How did His promises give you courage and strength?

3. Consider the practical implications for your daily walk with God. In what areas do you need to grow in courage and trust in His promises?

4. How can you overcome fear through trust in God's promises?

5. How does Joshua 1:9 inspire you to live with courage and resilience in your Christian journey, trusting in God's faithfulness and sovereignty?

Daniel 9:14 offers insight into God's righteous judgment and the consequences of disobedience. It highlights the importance of recognizing God's sovereignty, justice, and mercy in our lives. This study will help us understand the seriousness of disobedience and the hope found in repentance and God's faithfulness. If you have not read the full book of Daniel recently, take some time in the next few weeks and read through it – it is a powerful book in the Bible.

The Book of Daniel

The Book of Daniel is a prophetic book that combines historical narrative with visions of the future. It is set during the Babylonian exile of the Israelites and includes accounts of Daniel's faithfulness to God amidst challenging circumstances. Daniel 9 is particularly notable for its prayer of confession and the prophecy of the seventy weeks.

Immediate Context

Daniel 9 begins with Daniel studying the writings of the prophet Jeremiah and realizing that the desolation of Jerusalem would last seventy years. Moved by this revelation, Daniel prays a heartfelt prayer of confession, acknowledging the sins of Israel and seeking God's mercy. Daniel 9:14 is part of this prayer, where Daniel acknowledges God's righteousness in allowing the calamities that befell Israel due to their disobedience.

Exploring Daniel 9:14

The Text

"The LORD did not hesitate to bring the disaster on us, for the LORD our God is righteous in everything he does; yet we have not obeyed him" (Daniel 9:14, NIV).

Key Phrases

1. **"The LORD did not hesitate to bring the disaster on us"**

   o This phrase acknowledges God's swift action in bringing judgment upon Israel due to their persistent disobedience and rebellion against Him.

2. **"For the LORD our God is righteous in everything he does"**

   o This affirms God's righteousness and justice. Despite the severity of the judgment, God's actions are always just and right.

3. **"Yet we have not obeyed him"**

- This confession highlights Israel's failure to obey God's commandments, leading to the consequences they are experiencing. **Are you obeying God's commands?**

Theological Implications

God's Righteous Judgment

Daniel 9:14 shows that God's judgments are always righteous and just. His actions are never random but are responses to human behavior and the choices people make.

The Consequences of Disobedience

The verse serves as a reminder that disobedience to God's commands carries serious consequences. It underscores the importance of living in accordance with God's will and instructions.

The Need for Repentance

Acknowledging God's righteousness and our own disobedience is the first step toward repentance. Daniel's prayer exemplifies the humility and remorse required to seek God's forgiveness and restoration.

Practical Applications

Recognizing God's Justice

Believers should acknowledge God's justice and righteousness in all His actions. Understanding that God's judgments are fair and deserved helps us to trust Him even in difficult times.

Examining Our Lives

Daniel 9:14 encourages us to examine our own lives for areas of disobedience and sin. Regular self-reflection and confession are crucial for maintaining a right relationship with God.

Seeking God's Mercy

The verse teaches us the importance of seeking God's mercy through prayer and repentance. Even when we face the consequences of our actions, God's grace and forgiveness are quickly available to those who turn back to Him.

Misunderstandings and Cautions

Misinterpreting Divine Judgment

It is important not to misinterpret all suffering or disaster as direct punishment from God. While some consequences may be due to disobedience, not all hardships are divine judgments. Discernment and seeking God's wisdom are necessary.

Overlooking God's Mercy

Focusing solely on God's judgment can lead to fear and despair. It is essential to balance this understanding with the knowledge of God's mercy, grace, and readiness to forgive those who repent.

Ignoring Personal Responsibility

Blaming external circumstances for our mistakes prevents us from taking responsibility for our actions. Recognizing our faults and seeking repentance is vital for spiritual growth and reconciliation with God.

Biblical Examples

The Fall of Jerusalem

The fall of Jerusalem to the Babylonians, as described in 2 Kings 25, exemplifies the consequences of persistent disobedience to God. The destruction and exile were the fulfillment of God's warnings through the prophets about the judgment that would come due to Israel's unfaithfulness.

Jonah and Nineveh

The story of Jonah and Nineveh (Jonah 3-4) illustrates the power of repentance. When Jonah finally obeyed God's command to preach to the city of Nineveh, the people repented, and God relented from bringing disaster upon them, showcasing His mercy in response to genuine repentance.

King David's Repentance

King David's sin with Bathsheba and the following events (2 Samuel 11-12) demonstrate both the consequences of sin and the power of repentance. When confronted by the prophet Nathan, David confessed his sin and sought God's forgiveness, resulting in God's mercy, although there were still consequences for his actions.

Conclusion

Daniel 9:14 provides a thoughtful understanding of God's righteous judgment and the importance of obedience to His commands. Christians are called to acknowledge our disobedience, repent, and strive to live in accordance with God's will. Through this process, we experience God's forgiveness and grow in our relationship with Him, reflecting His righteousness and justice in our lives.

Brand 316 Inc www.brand316.org 727 North Waco #290 Wichita KS 67203 (316) 247-2050

Reflective Questions – Answer in Writing

1. How does recognizing God's justice and righteousness influence your view of the challenges and consequences you face in life?

2. What steps can you take to regularly examine your life for areas of disobedience and seek God's forgiveness?

3. How can understanding the balance between God's judgment and mercy help you in your spiritual journey?

4. Reflect on a time when you experienced the consequences of disobedience. How did you respond, and what did you learn from that experience?

5. How can you share the message of God's justice and mercy with others, encouraging them to seek His forgiveness and transformation?

Week 8: Abraham – The Father of Faith

Abraham, often referred to as the father of faith, embarked on a remarkable journey guided by his unwavering trust in God's promises. From leaving his homeland to the birth of his long-awaited son Isaac, Abraham's life is a testament to the power of faith and obedience. In this lesson, we will jump into the life of Abraham, exploring his strengths, weaknesses, and the ways in which God used him for His glory.

Verse to Review: Genesis 12:1-3

"The Lord had said to Abram, 'Go from your country, your people and your father's household to the land I will show you. I will make you into a great nation, and I will bless you; I will make your name great, and you will be a blessing. I will bless those who bless you, and whoever curses you I will curse; and all peoples on earth will be blessed through you.'"

History of Abraham:

Abraham, originally named Abram, was born in Ur of the Chaldeans. God called Abraham to leave his homeland and journey to a land that God would show him. In obedience, Abraham departed with his wife Sarah and nephew Lot, embarking on a journey of faith that would ultimately lead to the fulfillment of God's covenant promises.

Abraham's Strengths and Flaws:

Abraham's greatest strength was his unwavering faith and obedience to God. Despite facing numerous trials and uncertainties, Abraham trusted in God's promises and followed His lead without hesitation. Abraham's faithfulness earned him the title of "friend of God" and secured his place as the patriarch of the nation of Israel. However, Abraham also had his flaws, including moments of doubt and impatience.

Despite his overall faithfulness, Abraham sometimes struggled with doubt and impatience as he waited for God's promises to be fulfilled. When God's promise of a son seemed delayed, Abraham and Sarah took matters into their own hands, leading to the birth of Ishmael through Sarah's servant Hagar. This act of impatience caused strife within Abraham's household and had lasting consequences.

Abraham's lack of transparency regarding Sarah's identity as his wife led to misunderstandings and potentially dangerous situations. On two occasions, Abraham presented Sarah as his sister to foreign rulers out of fear for his own safety, resulting in potential threats to Sarah's honor and well-being (Genesis 12:10-20; 20:1-18). Abraham's failure to fully trust in God's protection and provision led to deception and compromised integrity.

Brand 316 Inc www.brand316.org 727 North Waco #290 Wichita KS 67203 (316) 247-2050

At times, Abraham struggled with fear and uncertainty, particularly when faced with threats from foreign rulers or uncertainties about God's plans. Despite God's repeated assurances of protection and blessing, Abraham's fear occasionally led him to compromise his integrity and trust in God's sovereignty.

God's Redemption Through Abraham's Faith:

Despite Abraham's flaws and moments of weakness, God remained faithful to His covenant promises and ultimately fulfilled them in His perfect timing. Through Abraham's faithfulness and obedience, God established a covenant with him, promising to bless him and make him the father of many nations. Despite the challenges and uncertainties Abraham faced, God remained faithful to His promises and used Abraham to bless all the nations of the earth.

Conclusion:

Abraham's life serves as a powerful example of faithfulness and obedience in the face of uncertainty and adversity. Despite his flaws and moments of doubt, Abraham remained steadfast in his commitment to follow God's lead and trust in His promises. Through his faithfulness, God established a covenant with Abraham, promising to bless him and make him the father of many nations.

One of the most significant lessons we can learn from Abraham's life is the importance of trusting in God's sovereignty and provision, even in the midst of uncertainty and doubt. Despite the challenges Abraham faced, including the delay in the fulfillment of God's promise of a son, Abraham remained faithful to God and obedient to His commands. Abraham's example challenges us to develop a similar spirit of obedience and trust in God's guidance in our own lives, knowing that He is faithful to fulfill His promises in His perfect timing.

Abraham's legacy of faithfulness and obedience endured beyond his lifetime, serving as an inspiration to future generations to trust in God's promises and follow His lead. Through his unwavering faith, Abraham became the father of many nations and a vessel of God's blessing to all the peoples of the earth. His example serves as a reminder of the transformative power of faith and obedience in fulfilling God's purposes and bringing about His kingdom on earth.

As we reflect on Abraham's story, may we be challenged to examine our own hearts and lives before God. May we, like Abraham, trust in God's promises and follow His lead, knowing that He is faithful to fulfill His purposes in our lives. And may we cultivate a spirit of faithfulness and obedience, knowing that God is faithful to reward those who seek Him with sincerity and devotion.

Abraham's life is a journey of faith and promise, marked by unwavering trust in God's sovereignty and provision. Despite his flaws and moments of weakness, Abraham remained faithful to God's call and obedient to His commands, ultimately becoming the father of many nations. As we reflect on Abraham's story, may we be challenged to examine our own hearts and lives before God. May we, like Abraham, trust in God's promises and follow His lead, knowing that He is faithful to fulfill His purposes in our lives.

Reflective Questions - Answer in Writing

1. In what ways do Abraham's strengths and weaknesses resonate with your own experiences and struggles?

2. Reflect on a time when you struggled with doubt or impatience in your faith journey. How did you overcome these challenges?

3. Consider Abraham's willingness to leave his homeland and journey to a land that God would show him. How can we cultivate a similar spirit of obedience and trust in God's guidance in our own lives?

4. Despite his flaws, Abraham remained faithful to God's call and obedient to His commands. How does Abraham's story give you hope for your own journey of faith?

5. How can you trust in God's promises and follow His lead, like Abraham, in your own relationship with God?

Week 9: Patience in Life from a Biblical Perspective

Patience is a quality often celebrated in both secular and religious contexts, yet it remains one of the most challenging qualities to cultivate. In a world where instant gratification is the norm, the biblical call to patience seems counter-cultural. However, patience is essential for making wise decisions, building strong relationships, growing in life and faith.

Biblical Foundation for Patience

The Bible provides numerous references that highlight the significance of patience. It is portrayed as a fruit of the Spirit, a mark of maturity, and a testament to one's faith in God's timing and sovereignty.

Patience as a Fruit of the Spirit

Galatians 5:22-23 (NIV) lists patience as one of the fruits of the Spirit: "But the fruit of the Spirit is love, joy, peace, forbearance, kindness, goodness, faithfulness, gentleness and self-control." Forbearance, often translated as patience, is an essential characteristic of a Spirit-filled life. It reflects the presence of the Holy Spirit working within us, enabling us to withstand challenges with grace.

Patience in Trials

James 1:2-4 (NIV) underscores the value of patience during trials: "Consider it pure joy, my brothers and sisters, whenever you face trials of many kinds, because you know that the testing of your faith produces perseverance. Let perseverance finish its work so that you may be mature and complete, not lacking anything." Trials are opportunities for growth, and patience is the key to emerging stronger and more mature in faith.

Patience in Decision-Making

Proverbs 19:2 (NIV) warns against hasty decisions: "Desire without knowledge is not good—how much more will hasty feet miss the way!" Making decisions in haste (not fully thought through or in a rush) often leads to mistakes and regrets. Patience allows time for careful consideration, seeking God's guidance, and ensuring that our choices align with His will.

The Role of Patience in Decision-Making

Patience plays a crucial role in making wise and informed decisions. It helps us to wait for the right time, seek advice and avoid impulsive actions that could lead to negative consequences.

Waiting for God's Timing

Ecclesiastes 3:1 (NIV) states, "There is a time for everything, and a season for every activity under the heavens." God's timing is perfect, and waiting for His direction ensures that our actions are in line with

His plan. Abraham and Sarah's story is a powerful example of the importance of waiting on God's timing. Their impatience led to complications when they tried to fulfill God's promise of a son through their own means (Genesis 16). In contrast, waiting for God's promise to be fulfilled through Isaac brought blessings (Genesis 21).

Seeking Guidance

Proverbs 15:22 (NIV) says, "Plans fail for lack of counsel, but with many advisers they succeed." Patience allows us to seek wise advice and gather necessary information before making decisions. This helps to ensure that our choices are well-informed and guided by wisdom.

Avoiding Impulsivity

Proverbs 14:29 (NIV) highlights the value of patience in controlling anger and avoiding rash choices: "Whoever is patient has great understanding, but one who is quick-tempered displays folly." Impulsive decisions, often driven by emotions like anger or frustration, can lead to negative outcomes. Patience helps us remain calm, think clearly, and make rational decisions.

Steps in Developing Patience

Improving patience requires intentional effort and reliance on God's grace. Here are some practical steps to develop patience in our lives.

Prayer and Meditation

Philippians 4:6-7 (NIV) encourages us to bring our concerns to God in prayer: "Do not be anxious about anything, but in every situation, by prayer and petition, with thanksgiving, present your requests to God. And the peace of God, which transcends all understanding, will guard your hearts and your minds in Christ Jesus." Regular prayer and meditation on God's Word help to promote a peaceful and patient heart.

Reflecting on God's Patience

2 Peter 3:9 (NIV) reminds us of God's patience with humanity: "The Lord is not slow in keeping his promise, as some understand slowness. Instead he is patient with you, not wanting anyone to perish, but everyone to come to repentance." Reflecting on God's patience with us can inspire us to be patient with ourselves and others.

Practicing Patience in Small Things

Luke 16:10 (NIV) states, "Whoever can be trusted with very little can also be trusted with much, and whoever is dishonest with very little will also be dishonest with much." Practicing patience in everyday situations, like waiting in line or dealing with inconveniences, helps us build patience for larger and unexpected challenges.

Relying on the Holy Spirit

Romans 8:26 (NIV) assures us of the Holy Spirit's help: "In the same way, the Spirit helps us in our weakness. We do not know what we ought to pray for, but the Spirit himself intercedes for us through wordless groans." Relying on the Holy Spirit strengthens our ability to be patient, especially in difficult circumstances.

Biblical Examples of Patience

The Bible is full of examples of people who demonstrated remarkable patience, providing us with valuable lessons.

Job

Job's story is a profound example of patience in suffering. Despite losing his wealth, health, and family, Job remained steadfast in his faith. Job 1:21 (NIV) records his response: "The Lord gave and the Lord has taken away; may the name of the Lord be praised." Job's patience was rewarded when God restored his fortunes and blessed him even more abundantly (Job 42:10-17).

Joseph

Joseph's journey from being sold into slavery to becoming the second most powerful man in Egypt is a testament to patience and trust in God's plan. Despite the injustices he faced, Joseph remained faithful and patient. Genesis 50:20 (NIV) captures his perspective: "You intended to harm me, but God intended it for good to accomplish what is now being done, the saving of many lives."

David

David, anointed as king at a young age, waited many years before actually ascending to the throne. During this time, he faced numerous challenges, including being pursued by King Saul. David's patience and trust in God's timing are evident in Psalm 27:14 (NIV): "Wait for the Lord; be strong and take heart and wait for the Lord."

The Rewards of Patience

Patience produces numerous benefits, both spiritually and practically. It leads to better decision-making, stronger relationships, and deeper spiritual growth.

Better Decision-Making

Proverbs 21:5 (NIV) says, "The plans of the diligent lead to profit as surely as haste leads to poverty." Patience allows us to make thoughtful and informed decisions, avoiding the pitfalls of impulsive actions.

Stronger Relationships

Colossians 3:12-13 (NIV) highlights the role of patience in maintaining healthy relationships: "Therefore, as God's chosen people, holy and dearly loved, clothe yourselves with compassion, kindness, humility, gentleness and patience. Bear with each other and forgive one another if any of you has a grievance against someone. Forgive as the Lord forgave you." Patience creates understanding, forgiveness, and harmony in relationships.

Deeper Spiritual Growth

Romans 5:3-4 (NIV) illustrates how patience contributes to spiritual maturity: "Not only so, but we also glory in our sufferings, because we know that suffering produces perseverance; perseverance, character; and character, hope." Patience in trials strengthens our character and deepens our hope in God.

Conclusion

Patience is an essential characteristic for living a Christ-centered life. It plays a critical role in making wise decisions, building strong relationships, and growing spiritually. By understanding the biblical foundation for patience, recognizing its role in decision-making, and practicing it intentionally, we develop this vital quality. Reflecting on biblical examples of patience and relying on the Holy Spirit will further strengthen our ability to be patient in all circumstances.

Reflective Questions – Answer in Writing

1. How can you apply the principle of waiting for God's timing in your current life decisions? Reflect on specific situations where patience is needed.

2. What are some practical steps you can take to seek wise counsel before making important decisions?

Brand 316 Inc www.brand316.org 727 North Waco #290 Wichita KS 67203 (316) 247-2050

3. How can you practice patience in your everyday interactions and relationships? Identify areas where you struggle with impatience.

4. Reflect on a time when being patient led to a positive outcome. How can this experience encourage you to be more patient in the future?

5. In what ways can you rely more on the Holy Spirit to help you develop patience?

Week 10: James 3:16 - 17 - Pursuing Godly Wisdom and Peace

James 3:16 is a verse that sheds light on the consequences of harboring envy and selfish ambition. It warns believers about the chaos and evil that arise from such attitudes and emphasizes the need for wisdom that promotes peace and righteousness. This study will help guide us to recognize and address harmful attitudes while seeking godly wisdom.

The Book of James

The Book of James is known for its practical teachings on Christian living. Written by James, the brother of Jesus, this epistle addresses the behavior and attitudes that should characterize believers. It covers topics such as faith and works, taming the tongue, and the dangers of worldliness.

Immediate Context

James 3 focuses on the power of the tongue and the nature of true wisdom. Verses 13-18 contrast earthly wisdom with heavenly wisdom. James describes how envy and selfish ambition lead to disorder and evil practices, while godly wisdom brings peace, mercy, and good fruit.

Exploring James 3:16

The Text

"For where you have envy and selfish ambition, there you find disorder and every evil practice" (James 3:16, NIV).

Key Phrases

1. **"Where you have envy and selfish ambition"**

   o This phrase identifies the root causes of disorder and evil practices. Envy and selfish ambition stem from a self-centered mindset and a desire for personal gain at the expense of others.

2. **"There you find disorder and every evil practice"**

   o This highlights the consequences of harboring envy and selfish ambition. Such attitudes lead to chaos, conflict, and immoral behavior within communities and relationships.

Theological Implications

The Dangers of Envy and Selfish Ambition

James 3:16 warns that envy and selfish ambition are destructive forces. These attitudes disrupt harmony, breed conflict, and give rise to various forms of evil. Recognizing and addressing these attitudes is crucial for maintaining healthy, godly relationships.

The Need for Godly Wisdom

The verse indirectly points to the importance of seeking godly wisdom, which contrasts with the earthly wisdom driven by selfish desires. Godly wisdom promotes peace, humility, and righteousness, creating a community that reflects Christ's love and character. You gain Godly wisdom through prayer and studying the Bible – the Word of God.

The Role of the Heart

James 3:16 emphasizes that the root of disorder and evil practices lies in the heart's attitudes. Transforming our hearts through the Holy Spirit and aligning our desires with God's will is essential for overcoming envy and selfish ambition.

Practical Applications

Self-Examination

Regularly examine your heart for traces of envy and selfish ambition. Ask the Holy Spirit to reveal any areas where these attitudes may be taking root and seek God's help in addressing them.

Developing Godly Wisdom

Pursue godly wisdom by immersing yourself in God's Word, seeking His guidance through prayer, and surrounding yourself with wise and Christian influences. Aim to develop attitudes that reflect humility, peace, and a desire to serve others.

Promoting Peace and Unity

Actively work to promote peace and unity within your community. Address conflicts with humility and seek reconciliation. Encourage others to embrace godly wisdom and reject attitudes that lead to division and conflict.

Misunderstandings and Cautions

Ignoring Subtle Forms of Envy and Ambition

Envy and selfish ambition can manifest subtly, making them difficult to recognize. Be vigilant in examining your motivations and attitudes, even in seemingly small matters.

Overlooking the Role of Godly Wisdom

Focusing solely on the negative aspects of envy and ambition without seeking godly wisdom can lead to a sense of hopelessness. Remember that God offers wisdom and guidance to those who seek it, enabling us to overcome destructive attitudes.

Failing to Address Root Causes

Addressing the symptoms of envy and ambition without tackling their root causes in the heart can lead to temporary solutions. Seek genuine heart transformation through a deep relationship with God and the work of the Holy Spirit. Pray often!

Biblical Examples

Cain and Abel

In Genesis 4:1-16, Cain's envy of Abel led to the first murder recorded in the Bible. Cain's selfish ambition and jealousy resulted in the ultimate act of disorder and evil practice. This story illustrates the destructive power of unchecked envy.

The Disciples' Ambition

In Mark 10:35-45, James and John asked Jesus for positions of honor in His kingdom. Their ambition caused discord among the disciples. Jesus used this moment to teach them about true greatness, which is found in serving others, not seeking power.

Korah's Rebellion

In Numbers 16, Korah, driven by selfish ambition, led a rebellion against Moses and Aaron. His desire for power and recognition resulted in chaos and severe consequences for him and his followers. This account demonstrates the dangers of ambition and the importance of respecting God's appointed leadership.

Conclusion

James 3:16 offers a sobering reminder of the consequences of harboring envy and selfish ambition. Christians are called to pursue godly wisdom, which promotes peace, humility, and righteousness. Through self-examination, developing godly wisdom, and promoting peace, we can create communities that reflect Christ's love and character.

Reflective Questions – Answer in Writing

1. How can you identify and address subtle forms of envy and selfish ambition in your life?

2. What steps can you take to develop godly wisdom and align your attitudes with God's will? List the steps out so you can easily follow them.

3. How can you actively promote peace and unity within your current situation, especially in situations of conflict?

4. Reflect on a time when envy or ambition caused disorder in your life or relationships. How did you respond, and what did you learn from that experience?

5. How can you encourage others to seek godly wisdom and reject attitudes that lead to division and strife?

Week 11: Ecclesiastes 3:16 - The Search for Justice and Injustice

Ecclesiastes 3:16 presents a sobering observation about the presence of wickedness in places where justice and righteousness should prevail. This verse invites us to reflect on the realities of injustice in the world and challenges us to seek God's wisdom and justice. This should help us understand how to navigate a world marked by imperfection and injustice.

The Book of Ecclesiastes

Ecclesiastes is part of the wisdom literature in the Old Testament, traditionally attributed to King Solomon. The book explores profound questions about the meaning of life, the pursuit of happiness, and the inevitability of death. It often presents a perspective of life "under the sun," emphasizing the futility and vanity of human endeavors without a proper understanding of God's sovereignty.

Immediate Context

Ecclesiastes 3 is well-known for its poetic reflection on the different seasons of life ("a time for everything"). Verses 1-8 outline the various times and seasons that characterize human existence. Verse 16 shifts focus to the observation of injustice and wickedness in places where one would expect to find justice and righteousness.

Exploring Ecclesiastes 3:16

The Text

"And I saw something else under the sun: In the place of judgment—wickedness was there, in the place of justice—wickedness was there" (Ecclesiastes 3:16, NIV).

Key Phrases

1. **"And I saw something else under the sun"**

   - The phrase "under the sun" refers to life in the natural, human world, emphasizing the earthly perspective of the writer's observations.

2. **"In the place of judgment—wickedness was there"**

   - This points to the presence of corruption and injustice within judicial systems and places where fair judgment should be rendered.

3. **"In the place of justice—wickedness was there"**

   - This highlights the pervasiveness of wickedness even in institutions designed to uphold justice and righteousness, reflecting the fallen state of the world.

Theological Implications

The Reality of Injustice

Ecclesiastes 3:16 acknowledges the harsh reality that injustice exists even in places where justice should prevail. This observation is a candid acknowledgment of the fallen and imperfect nature of human systems and institutions.

Human Limitations

The verse underscores human limitations in achieving perfect justice. It reveals the need for divine intervention and the ultimate justice that only God can provide.

God's Sovereignty

While Ecclesiastes often reflects on life's vanities and injustices, it ultimately points to God's sovereignty and the hope that He will bring about perfect justice in His time. Trusting in God's wisdom and timing is crucial for believers.

Practical Applications

Recognizing Injustice

Believers are called to recognize and acknowledge the presence of injustice in the world. This awareness should prompt us to seek God's wisdom and guidance in addressing and responding to injustice.

Pursuing Righteousness

Despite the presence of wickedness, Christians are called to pursue righteousness and justice in their own lives and communities. This involves standing up for what is right, advocating for the oppressed, and acting with integrity.

Trusting in God's Justice

While human efforts to achieve justice are important, ultimate justice belongs to God. Trusting in His sovereignty and timing provides hope and perspective when faced with the injustices of the world.

Misunderstandings and Cautions

Doubt and Despair

The recognition of widespread injustice can lead to cynicism and despair. It is important to balance this awareness with the hope and trust in God's ultimate justice and plan.

Passive Acceptance

Brand 316 Inc www.brand316.org 727 North Waco #290 Wichita KS 67203 (316) 247-2050

Acknowledging that injustice exists should not lead to passive acceptance. Believers are called to actively work towards justice and righteousness while trusting in God's ultimate sovereignty.

Misplaced Trust

Relying solely on human systems for justice can be misleading. Believers should place their ultimate trust in God's perfect justice and seek His guidance in addressing earthly injustices.

Biblical Examples

The Prophets and Social Justice

The Old Testament prophets, such as Isaiah and Amos, often spoke out against social injustice and corruption among leaders and judges. They called God's people to repentance and righteousness, emphasizing God's concern for justice.

- **Isaiah 1:17**: "Learn to do right; seek justice. Defend the oppressed. Take up the cause of the fatherless; plead the case of the widow."

- **Amos 5:24**: "But let justice roll on like a river, righteousness like a never-failing stream!"

Jesus and the Money Changers

In John 2:13-16, Jesus drives out the money changers from the temple, condemning their corrupt practices. This act demonstrates Jesus' commitment to justice and righteousness, challenging corruption in a place meant for worship.

The Early Church and Fairness

In Acts 6:1-7, the early church addresses complaints about the unfair distribution of food to widows. The apostles appoint seven men to ensure fair and just distribution, reflecting the church's commitment to addressing injustice and maintaining righteousness within the community.

Conclusion

Ecclesiastes 3:16 offers a realistic view of the presence of injustice in the world, even in places where justice should prevail. We are called to recognize and address injustice, pursue righteousness, and trust in God's ultimate justice.

Reflective Questions - Answer in Writing

1. How do you perceive the presence of injustice in your own community or society? How can you address it in practical ways?

2. In what ways can you pursue righteousness and justice in your personal life and interactions with others?

3. How does trusting in God's ultimate justice influence your perspective on the injustices you observe in the world?

4. Reflect on a time when you witnessed or experienced injustice. How did it affect you, and how did you respond?

5. How can Churches work together to address and combat injustice, reflecting God's love and righteousness to the world?

Week 12: Adam: The First Man and the fall of Humanity

Adam, the first man created by God, occupies a central role in the biblical narrative as the progenitor of humanity and the representative head of the human race. His story, recorded in the book of Genesis, serves as the foundational account of creation, the origin of sin, and the need for redemption. In this lesson, we will explore the life of Adam, examining his strengths, weaknesses, and the profound implications of his actions for all humanity.

Verse to Review: Genesis 2:7

"Then the Lord God formed a man from the dust of the ground and breathed into his nostrils the breath of life, and the man became a living being."

Background of Adam:

Adam was created by God in the Garden of Eden, formed from the dust of the ground and imbued with the breath of life. He was given dominion over the earth and tasked with tending the garden and naming the animals. In addition, Adam enjoyed intimate fellowship with God, walking and communing with Him in the cool of the day. However, Adam's obedience to God's commands was tested when he was instructed not to eat from the tree of the knowledge of good and evil.

Strengths and Flaws of Adam:

Adam possessed both strengths and weaknesses that shaped his identity and destiny as the first man. Some of his strengths include:

1. **Stewardship of Creation:** Adam was entrusted with the responsibility of tending and caring for the Garden of Eden, exercising dominion over the animals and the earth. His role as caretaker reflected his status as the pinnacle of God's creation and the representative head of humanity.
2. **Intimate Relationship with God:** Adam enjoyed unbroken fellowship with God, walking and communing with Him in the garden. His relationship with God was characterized by intimacy, trust, and obedience, as evidenced by his willingness to follow God's commands and instructions. Take a minute and reflect on that, imagine that!
3. **Reflecting God's Image:** As the first man created in the image of God, Adam bore the divine imprint of his Creator, reflecting God's character and attributes in his nature and essence. His capacity for reasoning, creativity, and moral agency distinguished him from the rest of creation and endowed him with dignity and worth.

However, Adam also had his flaws and weaknesses:

1. **Disobedience and Sin:** Despite God's clear command not to eat from the tree of the knowledge of good and evil, Adam yielded to the temptation of the serpent and ate the forbidden fruit. His

58

disobedience resulted in the introduction of sin and death into the world, fracturing his relationship with God and plunging humanity into spiritual darkness and separation from God.

2. **Failure to Take Responsibility:** After eating the forbidden fruit, Adam attempted to shift the blame onto Eve and ultimately onto God Himself, refusing to take responsibility for his own actions. His failure to confess his sin and seek forgiveness further exacerbated the consequences of his disobedience and rebellion against God.

3. **Consequences of the Fall:** As a result of Adam's sin, the entire human race was plunged into a state of spiritual death and separation from God. The ground was cursed, and humanity was subjected to toil, pain and suffering. Adam's sin introduced a hereditary principle of sin and corruption into the human race, resulting in a universal condition of sinfulness and moral depravity.

God's Response to Adam:

Despite Adam's disobedience and rebellion, God did not abandon humanity to its fate but instead initiated a plan of redemption and reconciliation. He promised to send a Savior who would crush the head of the serpent and deliver humanity from the power of sin and death. Moreover, God clothed Adam and Eve with garments of skin, foreshadowing the atoning sacrifice of Jesus Christ, who would cover the shame and nakedness of humanity with His righteousness.

The story of Adam shows us the consequences of sin and the need for redemption. Adam's disobedience and rebellion against God resulted in the fall of humanity and the introduction of sin and death into the world. However, God's response to Adam's sin demonstrates His grace, mercy, and unfailing love for humanity, as evidenced by His provision of a Savior and His promise of redemption through the seed of the woman.

Conclusion:

The story of Adam and Eve in the Garden of Eden is not merely a historical account but a timeless allegory that speaks to the universal human experience of temptation, sin, and redemption. Adam's failure to obey God's command not only resulted in his own spiritual death and separation from God but also affected the entire human race, plunging humanity into a state of sin and alienation from God. However, even in the midst of judgment and condemnation, God's grace and mercy remained evident as He initiated a plan of redemption and reconciliation through the promised seed of the woman.

Moreover, Adam's story serves as a profound reminder of the importance of personal responsibility and accountability in the face of temptation and sin. Instead of owning up to his actions and seeking forgiveness, Adam attempted to shift the blame onto Eve and ultimately onto God Himself, refusing to acknowledge his own guilt and culpability. His failure to take responsibility for his sin only compounded the consequences of his disobedience and rebellion against God, highlighting the destructive power of pride and self-justification.

Furthermore, Adam's story underscores the foundational truth of the Christian faith regarding the doctrine of original sin and the need for a Savior. As the representative head of humanity, Adam's sin introduced a hereditary principle of sin and corruption into the human race, resulting in a universal condition of spiritual death and separation from God. However, God in His mercy provided a solution to the problem of sin through the person and work of Jesus Christ.

Adam's life offers valuable lessons for believers today, reminding us of the devastating consequences of sin and the need for redemption and reconciliation with God. His strengths and weaknesses serve as a sobering reminder of the frailty of human nature and the importance of obedience and trust in God's commands. As we reflect on Adam's story, may we be inspired to confess our sins, seek forgiveness and restoration, and embrace the hope of redemption and eternal life through faith in Jesus Christ.

Reflective Questions - Answer in Writing

1. In what ways do you see yourself in the strengths and weaknesses of Adam?

2. Reflect on a time when you yielded to temptation and disobeyed God's commands. How did this impact your relationship with God and others?

3. Consider the consequences of Adam's disobedience for humanity. How does this underscore the universal need for redemption and reconciliation with God?

4. Reflect on God's response to Adam's sin, including His promise of a Savior and His provision of atonement through the sacrificial system. How does this demonstrate God's grace and mercy toward humanity?

5. How does the story of Adam challenge you to confess your sins, seek forgiveness, and embrace the hope of redemption and reconciliation with God through faith in Jesus Christ?

Week 13: Romans 12:10-15 - Living in Love and Hospitality

Romans 12:10-15 offers practical instructions for living out the Christian faith in community. These verses emphasize the importance of love, humility, and empathy among believers. As Christians, we should do all we can to learn how to build a supportive and loving Christian community no matter our current situation.

The Book of Romans

The Book of Romans is one of Paul's epistles, written to the Christians in Rome. It is known for its comprehensive theological insights and practical instructions for living out the Christian faith. Paul wrote this letter to explain the gospel and its implications for both Jews and Gentiles.

Immediate Context

Romans 12 marks a shift from the doctrinal teachings in the earlier chapters to practical exhortations. Paul begins this chapter by urging believers to offer their bodies as living sacrifices and to be transformed by the renewing of their minds. Verses 10-15 provide specific instructions for how Christians should relate to one another and live out their faith in community.

Exploring Romans 12:10-15

The Text

"Be devoted to one another in love. Honor one another above yourselves. Never be lacking in zeal, but keep your spiritual fervor, serving the Lord. Be joyful in hope, patient in affliction, faithful in prayer. Share with the Lord's people who are in need. Practice hospitality. Bless those who persecute you; bless and do not curse. Rejoice with those who rejoice; mourn with those who mourn." (Romans 12:10-15, NIV)

Key Phrases

1. **"Be devoted to one another in love"**

   o   This phrase emphasizes the importance of a deep, familial love among believers, having strong and supportive relationships within the Christian community.

2. **"Honor one another above yourselves"**

   o   Paul calls for humility and selflessness, encouraging believers to put others' needs and honor above their own.

3. **"Never be lacking in zeal, but keep your spiritual fervor, serving the Lord"**

- Believers are urged to maintain enthusiasm and dedication in their service to the Lord, avoiding complacency.

4. **"Be joyful in hope, patient in affliction, faithful in prayer"**

   - This verse highlights three key attitudes for Christians: joy in hopeful anticipation, patience during trials, and steadfastness in prayer.

5. **"Share with the Lord's people who are in need. Practice hospitality"**

   - Paul instructs believers to be generous and welcoming, meeting the needs of fellow Christians and showing hospitality.

6. **"Bless those who persecute you; bless and do not curse"**

   - Christians are called to respond to persecution with kindness and blessings, reflecting Christ's teachings on loving enemies.

7. **"Rejoice with those who rejoice; mourn with those who mourn"**

   - Paul encourages empathy and solidarity, urging believers to share in each other's joys and sorrows.

Theological Implications

The Nature of Christian Love

The love described in these verses goes beyond mere affection; it is a committed, selfless, and active love that seeks the best for others. This love is a reflection of Christ's love for us and a fundamental aspect of Christian community.

The Call to Humility

Honoring others above ourselves requires humility and a willingness to serve. This attitude counters the self-centered tendencies of our human nature and aligns us with Christ's example of servant leadership.

The Importance of Perseverance

Maintaining zeal, joy, patience, and faithfulness in prayer highlights the need for perseverance in the Christian life. These qualities sustain us through trials and help us remain focused on our spiritual goals.

Generosity and Hospitality

Generosity and hospitality are vital expressions of Christian love. By meeting the needs of others and welcoming them into our lives, we demonstrate the practical outworking of our faith.

Responding to Persecution

Blessing those who persecute us is a radical call to love our enemies. This response reflects the power of the gospel and the example of Jesus, who prayed for His persecutors.

Empathy and Solidarity

Rejoicing and mourning with others fosters a deep sense of community and empathy. This practice helps believers support one another through various life experiences, strengthening the body of Christ.

Practical Applications

Devoted Love

Actively seek ways to show love and devotion to fellow believers. This can include acts of kindness, words of encouragement, and being present in times of need.

Practice Humility

Make a conscious effort to honor others above yourself. This might involve listening more than speaking, serving in unseen ways, or celebrating others' successes without jealousy.

Maintaining Spiritual Fervor

Stay committed to your spiritual disciplines, such as prayer, Bible study, and worship. Seek to serve the Lord with enthusiasm and dedication, avoiding spiritual complacency.

Being Joyful, Patient, and Faithful

Embrace a hopeful outlook, especially during difficult times. Practice patience in the face of trials and remain faithful in your prayer life, trusting God's timing and plans.

Sharing and Hospitality

Look for opportunities to share your resources with those in need. Open your home and heart to others, practicing hospitality and building community.

Responding to Persecution with Blessings

When faced with hostility or persecution, choose to respond with kindness and blessings. Pray for those who oppose you and seek ways to demonstrate Christ's love to them.

Empathizing with Others

Make an effort to connect with others in their joys and sorrows. Celebrate their successes and offer comfort during their struggles, fostering a supportive and empathetic community.

Brand 316 Inc www.brand316.org 727 North Waco #290 Wichita KS 67203 (316) 247-2050

Misunderstandings and Cautions

Misinterpreting Devoted Love

Devoted love does not mean tolerating harmful behavior or enabling sin. It involves loving others while also seeking their ultimate good, which sometimes requires difficult conversations or boundaries.

Misunderstanding Humility

Humility is not self-deprecation or thinking less of yourself but thinking of yourself less. It involves recognizing your worth in Christ while prioritizing the needs and honor of others.

Avoiding Spiritual Burnout

Maintaining spiritual fervor should not lead to burnout. Balance your zeal with rest and self-care, recognizing that sustainable service is essential for long-term faithfulness.

Biblical Examples

The Early Church

Acts 2:42-47 describes the early Christian community, which devoted themselves to teaching, fellowship, breaking of bread, and prayer. They shared everything, met each other's needs, and practiced hospitality, embodying the principles Paul outlines in Romans 12.

Stephen

In Acts 7, Stephen exemplifies zeal and faithfulness even unto death. He boldly proclaims the gospel and as he is being stoned, prays for his persecutors, embodying the call to bless those who persecute us.

Ruth and Naomi

The story of Ruth and Naomi in the Book of Ruth highlights devoted love and mutual support. Ruth's unwavering loyalty to Naomi and her willingness to share in her sorrow and journey to a new land exemplify the principles of empathy and solidarity.

Conclusion

Romans 12:10-15 gives instructions for living out the Christian faith in community and creating a supportive, loving, and vibrant Christian community. As Christians, we are called to love deeply, practice humility, maintain spiritual fervor, show generosity, respond to persecution with blessings, and empathize with others. Let us commit to living out these principles, reflecting Christ's love and building a strong, compassionate community.

Reflective Questions – Answer in Writing

1. How can you create a deeper sense of love and devotion to other Christians?

2. In what practical ways can you honor others above yourself in your daily interactions?

3. How can you maintain your spiritual intensity and avoid complacency in your faith journey?

4. What opportunities do you have to practice generosity and hospitality?

5. How can you respond to those who oppose or persecute you with blessings and kindness?

Deuteronomy 6:16 is a verse that teaches an important lesson about faith and trust in God. It warns against testing God and encourages believers to trust His guidance and provision. This study will explore the context, meaning, and application of Deuteronomy 6:16, helping us understand how it relates to our lives today.

The Book of Deuteronomy

The Book of Deuteronomy is the fifth book of the Bible, written by Moses. It contains a series of speeches given by Moses to the Israelites before they enter the Promised Land. Deuteronomy reiterates the laws given by God and emphasizes the importance of obedience and faithfulness.

Immediate Context

Deuteronomy 6 is a chapter that emphasizes the importance of loving and obeying God. It includes the famous Shema, a declaration of the oneness of God and the call to love Him with all our heart, soul, and strength (Deuteronomy 6:4-5). Verses 10-19 warn the Israelites against forgetting God when they experience prosperity in the Promised Land, urging them to remain faithful and obedient.

Exploring Deuteronomy 6:16

The Text

"Do not put the Lord your God to the test as you did at Massah" (Deuteronomy 6:16, NIV).

Key Phrases

1. **"Do not put the Lord your God to the test"**

   o   This phrase warns against challenging or doubting God's power, provision, or promises.

2. **"As you did at Massah"**

   o   This refers to an event in Exodus 17:1-7, where the Israelites quarreled and tested God by demanding water, doubting His care and provision.

Theological Implications

Trusting God's Provision

Deuteronomy 6:16 teaches us to trust in God's provision and care. Testing God implies doubt and lack of faith in His ability to provide for our needs. Instead, we are called to trust His goodness and faithfulness.

66

Obedience to God's Commands

This verse is part of a broader call to obedience. By not testing God, we show our trust and commitment to follow His commands, recognizing His authority and wisdom.

Avoiding Rebellion

Testing God is a form of rebellion, showing a lack of submission to His will. Deuteronomy 6:16 reminds us to maintain a posture of humility and trust, avoiding the rebellious attitude seen at Massah.

Practical Applications

Trusting God in Difficult Times

When we face challenges, it's easy to doubt God's provision and care. Deuteronomy 6:16 encourages us to trust God, even when circumstances are tough. We can rely on His past faithfulness as a foundation for our trust.

Faith in God's Promises

We should hold firmly to God's promises, believing that He will fulfill them in His perfect timing. This means not demanding signs or proofs from God but trusting His Word.

Avoiding Testing God

Testing God can manifest in various ways, such as setting conditions for our faith or demanding specific outcomes to believe in His power. Instead, we should develop a faith that trusts God's wisdom and timing without setting demands.

Misunderstandings and Cautions

Misinterpreting Trust

Trusting God doesn't mean passivity or ignoring practical steps. It means having faith in His overall plan while responsibly doing our part. For example, praying for provision while also working diligently.

Avoiding Presumption

We must not presume upon God's grace by engaging in risky or irresponsible behavior, expecting Him to rescue us regardless. Trusting God involves wise and faithful living.

Recognizing Testing vs. Seeking Guidance

There's a difference between testing God and seeking His guidance. It's important to ask for God's direction through prayer in our decisions while avoiding an attitude of skepticism or challenge.

Biblical Examples

The Israelites at Massah

In Exodus 17:1-7, the Israelites tested God by complaining about the lack of water, doubting His care despite witnessing many miracles. This event serves as a warning against doubting God's provision and testing His patience.

Jesus' Temptation

In Matthew 4:1-11, Jesus is tempted by Satan in the wilderness. Satan challenges Jesus to throw Himself down from the temple, quoting Scripture to justify it. Jesus responds with Deuteronomy 6:16, saying, "It is also written: 'Do not put the Lord your God to the test.'" Jesus exemplifies trust in God without demanding miraculous proof.

Conclusion

Deuteronomy 6:16 is a strong reminder to trust God fully and avoid testing Him. This verse teaches us to rely on God's provision, obey His commands, and avoid rebellion. By understanding the context, meaning, and practical applications of this verse, we can strengthen our faith and trust in God.

As Christians, we are called to trust in God's provision and promises, even in difficult times. By avoiding the temptation to test God, we demonstrate our faith and commitment to His will. Let us strive to live out the principles of Deuteronomy 6:16 in our daily lives, showing trust and obedience to our faithful and loving God.

Reflective Questions - Answer in Writing

1. Can you think of a specific time that you put God to the test? What would you have done differently?

2. Reflect on a time when you struggled to trust in God's faithfulness and provision. How did you overcome doubt and uncertainty?

3. In what specific areas do you need to grow trust and obedience in God?

4. How can you avoid the temptation to doubt God's care and provision? What are 3 steps you can take when making decisions?

5. How does Deuteronomy 6:16 inspire you to rely on God's promises and provision, even when faced with difficulties or trials?

Week 15: 1 Timothy 3:16 - The Mystery of Godliness Revealed

1 Timothy 3:16 summarizes the mystery and magnificence of the Christian faith. It provides a succinct summary of Jesus Christ's life, mission, and divine nature. This verse helps us grasp the foundational truths of our faith and the implications for our daily lives.

The Book of 1 Timothy

1 Timothy is an letter written by the Apostle Paul to Timothy, his young protégé and leader of the church in Ephesus. The letter contains instructions on church leadership, sound doctrine, and godly living, aiming to equip Timothy for effective ministry.

Immediate Context

In 1 Timothy 3, Paul outlines the qualifications for overseers and deacons in the church, emphasizing the importance of godly character and conduct. Verse 16 concludes the chapter with a poetic declaration of the mystery of godliness, summarizing key aspects of Jesus Christ's divine mission.

Exploring 1 Timothy 3:16

The Text

"Beyond all question, the mystery from which true godliness springs is great: He appeared in the flesh, was vindicated by the Spirit, was seen by angels, was preached among the nations, was believed on in the world, was taken up in glory." (1 Timothy 3:16, NIV)

Key Phrases

1. **"He appeared in the flesh"**

   o   This refers to the incarnation, the act of God becoming human in the person of Jesus Christ. It emphasizes the mystery of God's divine nature dwelling in human form.

2. **"Was vindicated by the Spirit"**

   o   This points to the Holy Spirit's role in affirming Jesus' divine nature, particularly through His resurrection from the dead, which proved His righteousness and divine sonship.

3. **"Was seen by angels"**

   o   This indicates the heavenly witnesses to Jesus' life and mission, including His birth, ministry, resurrection, and ascension.

4. **"Was preached among the nations"**

- This highlights the proclamation of the gospel to all peoples, fulfilling the Great Commission and spreading the message of salvation worldwide.

5. **"Was believed on in the world"**

- This phrase underscores the global acceptance of the gospel and the faith of countless believers throughout the ages.

6. **"Was taken up in glory"**

- This refers to Jesus' ascension into heaven, where He sits at the right hand of the Father, signifying His exaltation and eternal reign.

Theological Implications

The Mystery of Godliness

The "mystery" refers to the profound and previously hidden truths about God's plan of salvation, now revealed through Jesus Christ. This mystery is the foundation of true godliness, calling believers to a life transformed by these divine truths.

The Incarnation

Jesus' incarnation is a central doctrine of Christianity, demonstrating God's immense love and willingness to dwell among humanity. This act of divine humility and solidarity with humanity calls believers to live incarnationally, embodying Christ's love in the world.

The Role of the Holy Spirit

The Holy Spirit's vindication of Jesus through His resurrection assures believers of Jesus' divinity and the truth of His teachings. It also empowers believers to live godly lives, bearing witness to Christ's transformative power.

The Universal Proclamation

The preaching of the gospel to all nations signifies the inclusivity and universality of God's salvation plan. It challenges believers to participate in the mission of sharing the gospel and making disciples of all nations.

Faith and Belief

The widespread belief in the gospel underscores the power and truth of the Christian message. It encourages believers to hold fast to their faith and to continue spreading the good news.

The Ascension and Exaltation

Jesus' ascension and exaltation highlight His divine authority and eternal reign. It assures Christians of His ongoing presence and intercession and calls them to live with the hope of His return and the establishment of His kingdom.

Practical Applications

Embracing the Mystery

- **Reflect on the Incarnation**: Contemplate the significance of God becoming human in Jesus Christ. Let this truth deepen your appreciation for God's love and inspire you to live with humility and compassion.

- **Depend on the Holy Spirit**: Rely on the Holy Spirit for guidance, strength, and transformation. Seek His presence in your daily life and allow Him to shape your character and actions.

Proclaiming the Gospel

- **Share Your Faith**: Be bold in sharing the gospel with others. Look for opportunities to talk about Jesus and the difference He has made in your life.

- **Support Mission Work**: Engage in or support mission efforts that aim to spread the gospel to unreached peoples. Pray for missionaries and consider how you can contribute to their work.

Living with Hope

- **Focus on Christ's Return**: Live with the expectation and hope of Christ's return. Let this hope influence your decisions, priorities, and how you invest your time and resources.

- **Practice Godliness**: Strive to live a godly life, reflecting the character of Christ in your words and actions. Allow the truths of 1 Timothy 3:16 to shape your values and behaviors.

Misunderstandings and Cautions

Overlooking the Mystery

Do not take the profound truths of the Christian faith for granted. Regularly remind yourself of the mystery of godliness and let it inspire awe, worship, and devotion.

Neglecting the Universal Mission

Avoid becoming inward-focused and neglecting the call to share the gospel with others. Remember the global scope of God's salvation plan and your role in it.

Biblical Examples

The Early Church

The early church, as described in Acts, exemplified the principles in 1 Timothy 3:16. They preached the gospel to all nations, witnessed the Holy Spirit's power, and lived with the hope of Christ's return. Their faith and boldness led to the rapid spread of Christianity.

The Apostle Paul

Paul's life and ministry reflect a deep understanding of the mystery of godliness. He preached the gospel tirelessly, relied on the Holy Spirit, and lived with the hope of Christ's return. His letters provide rich theological insights and practical guidance for living out these truths.

The Thessalonian Church

The Thessalonian church, commended by Paul in 1 Thessalonians, exemplified faith, love, and hope. They received the gospel with joy, turned from idols to serve the living God, and eagerly awaited Christ's return. Their example encourages believers to live out the principles of 1 Timothy 3:16.

Conclusion

1 Timothy 3:16 offers a rich and concise summary of the core truths of the Christian faith. By understanding its meaning Christians can deepen their faith and commitment to living out these truths. We should embrace the mystery of godliness, proclaim the gospel and live with hope and godliness.

Reflective Questions – Answer in Writing

1. How does understanding the mystery of godliness deepen your faith and appreciation for God's love?

2. In what ways can you rely more on the Holy Spirit for guidance in your life?

3. When you think of the incarnation, what words come to your mind? How does it make you feel?

4. What practical steps can you take to live with the hope and expectation of Christ's return?

5. How do the truths of 1 Timothy 3:16 shape your values, priorities, and daily actions?

Week 16: Cain and Abel: The Consequences of Jealousy

The story of Cain and Abel, found in Genesis 4, is one of the earliest accounts of sibling rivalry and its tragic consequences. It serves as a cautionary tale about the destructive power of jealousy and the importance of faithfulness in worshiping God. In this lesson, we will explore the narrative of Cain and Abel, examining their actions, motivations, and the profound lessons we can learn from their story.

Verse to Review: Genesis 4:7

"If you do what is right, will you not be accepted? But if you do not do what is right, sin is crouching at your door; it desires to have you, but you must rule over it."

Background of Cain and Abel:

Cain and Abel were the sons of Adam and Eve, born after the expulsion from the Garden of Eden. As the first children born into a fallen world, they inherited the consequences of their parents' disobedience and the brokenness of human nature. Despite their shared heritage, Cain and Abel followed different paths in their worship of God, ultimately leading to tragedy.

Strengths and Flaws of Cain and Abel:

Cain and Abel's story reveals both their strengths and weaknesses, shedding light on their characters and choices. Some of their strengths include:

1. **Abel's Faithfulness:** Abel demonstrated faithfulness in his worship of God, offering the best of his flock as a sacrifice. His obedience and sincerity in bringing an acceptable offering to God reflected a heart that sought to honor and please God.
2. **Cain's Industry:** Cain was industrious and hardworking, cultivating the ground and offering *some* fruits of his labor as a sacrifice to God.
3. **Both Sons of Adam:** As descendants of Adam and Eve, Cain and Abel shared a common heritage and the potential for relationship with God. Their upbringing and environment provided opportunities for spiritual growth and obedience to God's commands.

However, Cain and Abel also had their flaws and weaknesses:

1. **Cain's Jealousy:** Cain's downfall stemmed from his jealousy and resentment towards Abel, whose offering was favored by God while his own was rejected. Instead of addressing his own shortcomings, Cain allowed jealousy to consume him, leading to anger, bitterness, and ultimately, violence. The text makes it clear that Abel brought "fat portions" while Cain brought "some" to God. It can be assumed that Cain's offering was not the best he had and minimal.
2. **Abel's Naivety:** While Abel's faithfulness in worshiping God was commendable, he may have been naive in failing to recognize the danger posed by Cain's jealousy and hostility. His

innocence and trust in his brother may have contributed to his vulnerability and tragic fate. Are there people in your life that you should evaluate if they have your best intentions at heart?

3. **Failure to Seek Reconciliation:** Both Cain and Abel failed to seek reconciliation and resolution of their conflict before it escalated to violence. Their inability to address their differences and reconcile with one another paved the way for tragedy and loss.

God's Response to Cain and Abel:

Despite their differences and the tragic outcome of their conflict, God showed mercy and grace towards Cain and Abel. He warned Cain of the consequences of his jealousy and urged him to master sin's desire to rule over him. Even after Cain committed the first murder by killing Abel, God marked him with a protective sign, sparing his life and offering him a chance for repentance. God did put Cain under a curse and said that he would be a restless wanderer on the earth.

The story of Cain and Abel serves as a sobering reminder of the consequences of sin and the importance of faithfulness in worshiping God. Cain's jealousy and Abel's faithfulness stand as stark contrasts, illustrating the choice between obedience and rebellion, blessing and curse. Ultimately, Cain's failure to rule over sin led to his downfall, while Abel's faithful sacrifice brought him into God's favor and memory. It is also clear in the text that God was first in Abel's life and was secondary in Cain's.

Conclusion:

The story of Cain and Abel offers valuable insights into the nature of sin and its consequences, as well as the importance of faithfulness and obedience in our relationship with God. Cain's jealousy and Abel's faithfulness serve as timeless reminders of the spiritual battle that rages within each of us, between the desires of the flesh and the call to righteousness. Like Cain, we are often tempted to give in to jealousy, anger, and resentment when things do not go our way or when others receive recognition and favor. However, the story of Cain and Abel challenges us to resist these temptations and instead choose the path of faithfulness, humility, and obedience to God's commands. It also shows that we serve a God of second chances.

Moreover, the story of Cain and Abel prompts us to examine the condition of our hearts and the motives behind our actions. Are we motivated by a desire to honor and please God, as Abel was, or are we driven by jealousy, pride, and selfish ambition, like Cain? The story of Cain and Abel reminds us that God sees not only our outward actions but also the thoughts and intentions of our hearts. He calls us to repentance and transformation, inviting us to turn away from sin and embrace the abundant life He offers through faith in Jesus Christ.

Furthermore, the story of Cain and Abel challenges us to seek reconciliation and resolution in our relationships, rather than allowing conflicts to fester and escalate. Cain's failure to address his jealousy and reconcile with Abel resulted in tragedy and loss, underscoring the importance of humility, forgiveness, and peacemaking in our interactions with others. As followers of Christ, we are called to be agents of reconciliation and healing in a broken and divided world, extending grace and mercy to those who have wronged us and seeking forgiveness from those we have wronged.

The story of Cain and Abel underscores the timeless truths of human nature and the consequences of our choices. Cain's jealousy and Abel's faithfulness serve as cautionary examples for us today, reminding us of the destructive power of sin and the importance of obedience in our relationship with God. **Before answering the questions, fully read the Genesis 4.**

Reflective Questions - Answer in Writing

1. In what ways do you see yourself in the characters of Cain and Abel?

2. Reflect on a time when jealousy or resentment clouded your judgment and led to negative consequences. How did you overcome these feelings?

3. Consider the importance of faithfulness in worshiping God, as demonstrated by Abel. How can we cultivate a heart that seeks to honor and please God in all we do?

4. Reflect on God's warning to Cain about sin's desire to rule over him. How can we guard our hearts against the destructive influence of sin in our lives?

5. How does the story of Cain and Abel challenge you to seek reconciliation and resolution in your relationships, rather than allowing conflicts to escalate?

Week 17: Revelation 3:16 – Examining Our Commitment to Christ

Revelation 3:16 is a powerful and convicting verse that challenges Christians to examine the focus of their faith and commitment to Christ. In this verse, Jesus addresses the church in Laodicea, rebuking them for their lukewarmness and calling them to a renewed passion and dedication.

The Book of Revelation

The Book of Revelation, written by the Apostle John, is a prophetic and apocalyptic text that contains visions and messages from Jesus Christ. It addresses the spiritual state of seven churches in Asia Minor and provides a glimpse into the ultimate victory of Christ over evil and the establishment of His eternal Kingdom.

Immediate Context

Revelation 3:16 is part of Jesus' message to the church in Laodicea, one of the seven churches mentioned in chapters 2 and 3. Laodicea was a wealthy and prosperous city known for its banking industry, textile production, and medical school. However, the church in Laodicea had become spiritually unworried, relying on their material wealth rather than on God.

Exploring Revelation 3:16

The Text

"So, because you are lukewarm—neither hot nor cold—I am about to spit you out of my mouth" (Revelation 3:16, NIV).

Key Phrases

1. **"Because you are lukewarm"**

   o   This phrase describes the spiritual condition of the Laodicean church. They were neither fervent (hot) nor completely indifferent (cold) but were apathetic and complacent.

2. **"Neither hot nor cold"**

   o   Being "hot" symbolizes fervent, passionate faith, while being "cold" represents a clear rejection of faith. Lukewarmness indicates a lack of commitment and zeal.

3. **"I am about to spit you out of my mouth"**

   o   This graphic expression signifies Jesus' strong disapproval and rejection of their lukewarmness. It highlights the seriousness of their spiritual state and the need for urgent change. Where do you stand in your faith?

77

Theological Implications

Spiritual Commitment

Revelation 3:16 emphasizes the importance of being passionate in our faith. Lukewarmness is unacceptable to God, as it reflects a lack of true commitment and zeal for Him.

God's Displeasure with Complacency

The verse shows that God desires wholehearted devotion and is deeply displeased with spiritual complacency. It serves as a warning that half-hearted faith can lead to rejection by God.

Call to Repentance

The strong language used by Jesus is intended to wake the Laodiceans from their complacency and call them to repentance and renewed commitment to Him.

Practical Applications

Evaluating Our Spiritual Temperature

As Christians, we should regularly assess our spiritual fervency. Are we passionate about our relationship with God, or have we become complacent and lukewarm? Honest self-examination can help us identify areas where we need to reignite our zeal for Christ. What steps can you take today to change that?

Renewing Our Commitment

If we find that we have become lukewarm, we must take steps to renew our commitment to God. This can involve spending more time in prayer and Bible study, engaging in acts of service and seeking fellowship with other believers who can encourage and challenge us.

Avoiding Complacency

We must guard against the dangers of spiritual satisfaction by continually seeking to grow in our faith and deepen our relationship with God. Regular spiritual disciplines and a heart of humility and dependence on God can help us maintain our passion.

Misunderstandings and Cautions

Misinterpreting "Hot" and "Cold"

Some may mistakenly believe that being "cold" is preferable to being "lukewarm." However, the context shows that both hot and cold are preferable to lukewarmness because they represent definitive spiritual states, whereas lukewarmness indicates indifference. **Read that again and evaluate where you are at!**

Ignoring the Call to Action

78

It is important not to ignore the call to action in this verse. Jesus' rebuke is meant to prompt change and renewal. We must not dismiss the seriousness of lukewarmness or fail to respond with repentance and renewed passion.

Biblical Examples

The Church in Ephesus

The church in Ephesus (Revelation 2:1-7) provides a contrast to Laodicea. While they were commended for their hard work and perseverance, they were warned for abandoning their first love. This serves as a reminder that action must be accompanied by a passionate love for Christ.

The Church in Smyrna

The church in Smyrna (Revelation 2:8-11) is another example. They were praised for their faithfulness despite suffering and poverty. Their faith and perseverance in the face of trials illustrate the kind of spiritual zeal that God desires.

The Church in Sardis

The church in Sardis (Revelation 3:1-6) was rebuked for having a reputation of being alive while being spiritually dead. Their smugness and lack of genuine faith highlight the dangers of resting on past achievements and neglecting a vibrant, ongoing relationship with God.

Conclusion

Revelation 3:16 is a powerful and sobering reminder of the importance of a wholehearted commitment to God. By understanding its context, meaning, and practical applications, we can be challenged to examine our own spiritual state and take steps to renew our zeal for Christ.

As Christians, we are called to avoid the dangers of lukewarmness and complacency, striving instead to maintain a passionate faith. Let us heed the warning of Revelation 3:16 and seek to grow in our relationship with God, living out our faith with zeal and dedication.

Reflective Questions - Answer in Writing

1. Honest Question and Answer – Are you Hot, Cold or Lukewarm? What steps can you take to improve your passion for Christ?

2. Reflect on a time when you may have been spiritually lukewarm. What steps did you take to overcome complacency and renew your commitment to Christ?

3. Consider the consequences being lukewarm. How do these consequences motivate you to pursue wholehearted devotion to Christ?

4. In what areas of your life do you need to repent and experience spiritual renewal? Be Specific

5. How can you develop love and devotion to Christ in your daily life, living with purpose and intentionality in all things?

Week 18: Isaiah 61:1-3 - The Spirit of the Lord's Anointing

Isaiah 61:1-3 is a powerful passage that speaks about God's mission to bring good news, healing, and freedom to those in need. It is a prophecy that finds its fulfillment in Jesus Christ, who quoted this passage at the beginning of His ministry.

The Book of Isaiah

The Book of Isaiah, written by the prophet Isaiah, contains prophecies that address both the immediate circumstances of Israel and future events, including the coming of the Messiah. Isaiah is known for its rich imagery and profound messages of hope, judgment, and restoration.

Immediate Context

Isaiah 61 is part of a section of the book that speaks about the restoration and redemption of Israel. It follows chapters that describe the suffering servant and the promises of comfort and salvation. Isaiah 61:1-3 specifically outlines the mission of the anointed one, who will bring God's salvation to His people.

Exploring Isaiah 61:1-3

The Text

"The Spirit of the Sovereign Lord is on me, because the Lord has anointed me to proclaim good news to the poor. He has sent me to bind up the brokenhearted, to proclaim freedom for the captives and release from darkness for the prisoners, to proclaim the year of the Lord's favor and the day of vengeance of our God, to comfort all who mourn, and provide for those who grieve in Zion—to bestow on them a crown of beauty instead of ashes, the oil of joy instead of mourning, and a garment of praise instead of a spirit of despair. They will be called oaks of righteousness, a planting of the Lord for the display of his splendor" (Isaiah 61:1-3, NIV).

Key Phrases

1. **"The Spirit of the Sovereign Lord is on me"**

   o This indicates that the speaker is empowered by God's Spirit to carry out a special mission.

2. **"Because the Lord has anointed me"**

   o Anointing signifies being chosen and set apart for a specific purpose. Here, it refers to the Messiah, whom God has appointed for a mission.

3. **"To proclaim good news to the poor"**

- The mission includes bringing hope and good news to those who are suffering or in need.

4. **"To bind up the brokenhearted"**

    - This means to heal and comfort those who are hurting.

5. **"To proclaim freedom for the captives and release from darkness for the prisoners"**

    - The mission involves setting people free from physical, emotional, and spiritual bondage.

6. **"To proclaim the year of the Lord's favor and the day of vengeance of our God"**

    - This refers to a time of God's grace and salvation, as well as His justice.

7. **"To comfort all who mourn"**

    - The mission includes providing comfort and hope to those who are grieving.

8. **"To bestow on them a crown of beauty instead of ashes"**

    - This symbolizes transformation and renewal, turning mourning into joy.

9. **"They will be called oaks of righteousness, a planting of the Lord for the display of his splendor"**

    - Those who receive God's salvation will be strong and righteous, displaying God's glory.

Theological Implications

The Mission of the Messiah

Isaiah 61:1-3 outlines the mission of the Messiah, who is empowered by the Holy Spirit to bring God's salvation. This mission includes preaching good news, healing the brokenhearted, freeing captives, and proclaiming God's favor and justice.

God's Compassion and Justice

This passage reveals God's deep compassion for the poor, brokenhearted, and oppressed. It also shows His commitment to justice and righteousness, promising both comfort and restoration.

Transformation and Renewal

God's mission through the Messiah includes transforming lives. He replaces mourning with joy, despair with praise, and ashes with beauty. This transformation is a powerful testimony to God's redemptive work.

Practical Applications

Embracing God's Mission

As followers of Christ, we are called to participate in God's mission. This means sharing the good news, comforting those who are hurting, and working for justice and freedom for the oppressed.

Finding Hope and Healing

Isaiah 61:1-3 offers hope and healing to those who are struggling. We can trust that God sees our pain and is at work to bring healing and restoration.

Living as Oaks of Righteousness

We are called to be "oaks of righteousness," displaying God's glory in our lives. This involves living out our faith in ways that reflect God's love, compassion, and justice.

Misunderstandings and Cautions

Expecting Immediate Transformation

While God's promise of transformation is real, it may not happen immediately or in the way we expect. We must trust God's timing and His process of working in our lives.

Ignoring the Call to Action

This passage calls us to action, not just to receive God's blessings but to be agents of His mission. We must be careful not to focus only on our own comfort and forget our responsibility to others.

Overlooking God's Justice

While the passage speaks of comfort and favor, it also mentions the "day of vengeance." God's justice is part of His character, and we must remember that His mission includes addressing sin and injustice.

Biblical Examples

Jesus Fulfills Isaiah 61:1-3

In Luke 4:16-21, Jesus reads Isaiah 61:1-2 in the synagogue and declares, "Today this scripture is fulfilled in your hearing." Jesus identifies Himself as the anointed one who brings good news, heals the brokenhearted, and sets captives free. His ministry reflects the mission outlined in Isaiah 61.

Modern-Day Application

Think of a Christian organization that helps the poor, such as a prison ministry, food pantry or a homeless shelter. These organizations embody the mission of Isaiah 61 by providing for those in need, offering hope, and working for justice. They are practical examples of how Christians can live out the call of this passage.

Conclusion

Isaiah 61:1-3 is a powerful passage that reveals God's mission to bring good news, healing, and freedom through the Messiah. This mission, fulfilled in Jesus, continues today as believers participate in God's work. By understanding the context, meaning, and practical applications of this passage, we can align our lives with God's mission and bring hope and healing to those around us.

As Christians, we are called to embrace God's mission, find hope and healing in His promises, and live as oaks of righteousness. This involves actively sharing the good news, comforting the brokenhearted, and working for justice. By doing so, we display God's glory and participate in His redemptive work in the world. Let us strive to live out the powerful truths of Isaiah 61:1-3 in our daily lives, bringing God's love and compassion to all we encounter.

Reflective Questions - Answer in Writing

1. How does Isaiah 61:1-3 challenge your understanding of the Messiah's mission and ministry?

2. How did this impact your perspective on God's heart for the broken and oppressed?

3. How can you actively respond to God's call to proclaim the good news, minister to the brokenhearted, and advocate for justice? Answer this for where you are at now along with where you will be in 10 years.

4. Think about the term "oaks of righteousness." Explain what picture that paints for you in your mind and how it can help you grow in Christ.

Week 19: 2 Peter 3:9 - The Patience and Promise of God

2 Peter 3:9 provides insights into God's character, particularly His patience and desire for everyone to come to repentance. This verse helps us understand God's timing and His merciful nature. It is important to encourage believers to reflect on God's patience and their response to His call to repentance.

The Book of 2 Peter

2 Peter is an epistle written by the Apostle Peter, addressing believers and warning them about false teachers and scoffers who challenge the truth of the gospel. Peter emphasizes the importance of growing in faith, knowledge, and godliness while awaiting Christ's return.

Immediate Context

In 2 Peter 3, Peter addresses the skepticism surrounding the promise of Christ's return. Scoffers were mocking the idea of Christ's second coming, arguing that everything has remained the same since the beginning of creation. Peter reminds believers of God's timing, emphasizing that God's delay is not a sign of forgetfulness but of His patience and desire for all to repent.

Exploring 2 Peter 3:9

The Text

"The Lord is not slow in keeping his promise, as some understand slowness. Instead, he is patient with you, not wanting anyone to perish, but everyone to come to repentance." (2 Peter 3:9, NIV)

Key Phrases

1. **"The Lord is not slow in keeping his promise, as some understand slowness"**

   o This phrase addresses the misconception that God is slow or negligent in fulfilling His promises. It emphasizes that God's timing is different from human expectations.

2. **"He is patient with you"**

   o God's patience is highlighted, indicating His long-suffering nature and willingness to give people time to repent.

3. **"Not wanting anyone to perish, but everyone to come to repentance"**

   o This reveals God's heart and desire for all people to be saved and to turn away from sin, underscoring His mercy and love.

Theological Implications

God's Patience

God's patience is an expression of His mercy and love. He delays judgment to provide more opportunities for people to repent and turn to Him. This patience should not be taken for granted but should lead to gratitude and repentance.

The Promise of Christ's Return

Christ's return is certain, but its timing is in God's hands. Believers are called to trust in God's promises and remain steadfast in their faith, even when it seems delayed.

Universal Call to Repentance

God desires everyone to come to repentance. This universal call reflects His inclusive love and the inclusivity of the gospel. It emphasizes that no one is beyond the reach of God's grace and forgiveness.

Practical Applications

Trusting God's Timing

- **Patience in Faith**: Trust in God's perfect timing, knowing that He is not slow but patient. This perspective helps believers endure and remain faithful during times of waiting.

- **Hopeful Expectation**: Live with hopeful expectation of Christ's return, allowing this hope to shape your actions and priorities.

Responding to God's Patience

- **Gratitude for Patience**: Be grateful for God's patience, recognizing it as an opportunity for repentance and growth.

- **Repentance and Renewal**: Regularly examine your life, confess sins, and seek God's forgiveness. Use God's patience as a motivation to repent and grow closer to Him.

Sharing the Message of Repentance

- **Evangelism**: Share the gospel with others, motivated by God's desire for everyone to come to repentance. Be a witness to God's love and patience.

- **Encouragement**: Encourage fellow believers to remain steadfast in their faith and to trust in God's promises, reminding them of God's patience and desire for all to be saved.

Misunderstandings and Cautions

Misinterpreting God's Patience

Avoid interpreting God's patience as a license to continue in sin. His patience is an opportunity for repentance, not an excuse for continuing in sinful behavior.

Scoffing at the Promise

Resist the temptation to doubt or scoff at the promise of Christ's return. Trust in God's faithfulness and His perfect timing, even when it seems delayed.

Biblical Examples

Noah's Generation

In Genesis 6-9, God's patience was evident during the time of Noah. Despite the wickedness of humanity, God waited and gave people time to repent while Noah built the ark. This story highlights both God's patience and the eventual fulfillment of His promise of judgment.

The Apostle Paul

Paul's life, as described in Acts 9 and his epistles, is a testament to God's patience and desire for repentance. Once a persecutor of Christians, Paul experienced a dramatic conversion and became a devoted follower of Christ. His story illustrates that no one is beyond the reach of God's grace.

Nineveh and Jonah

In the Book of Jonah, God sent Jonah to Nineveh to call its people to repentance. Despite Jonah's reluctance, the people of Nineveh repented, and God withheld His judgment. This narrative demonstrates God's patience and desire for all to turn from their wicked ways.

Conclusion

2 Peter 3:9 provides profound insights into God's character, emphasizing His patience, mercy, and desire for everyone to come to repentance. Christians should deepen their trust in God's promises and respond to His call for repentance. We are called to trust in God's timing, respond to His patience with gratitude and repentance, and share the message of the gospel with others.

Brand 316 Inc www.brand316.org 727 North Waco #290 Wichita KS 67203 (316) 247-2050

Reflective Questions – Answer in Writing

1. How does understanding God's patience change your perspective on His timing in your life?

2. In what areas of your life do you need to respond to God's patience with repentance?

3. How can you encourage others to trust in God's promises and His perfect timing?

4. What steps can you take to share the message of repentance and God's love with others?

5. How does the promise of Christ's return influence your daily actions and priorities?

Week 20: David: A Man After God's Own Heart

The story of David is one of triumph and tragedy, victory and failure. From humble beginnings as a shepherd boy to becoming the greatest king in Israel's history, David's life is a testament to the power of faith, repentance, and God's grace. In this lesson, we will explore the life of David, examining his strengths, weaknesses, and the ways in which God used him for His glory.

Verse to Review: Acts 13:22

"After removing Saul, he made David their king. God testified concerning him: 'I have found David son of Jesse, a man after my own heart; he will do everything I want him to do.'"

History of David:

David was the youngest son of Jesse, a shepherd from the tribe of Judah. Despite his humble origins, David was anointed by the prophet Samuel to be the future king of Israel while still a young man. David's journey to the throne was marked by numerous trials and challenges, including his conflict with King Saul and his exile from the land. Despite these hardships, David remained faithful to God and eventually ascended to the throne of Israel, where he ruled for forty years. David's story is well worth fully reading in the Bible and taking notes. You will find several similarities in his life compared to yours.

David's Strengths and Flaws:

David possessed many admirable qualities, including his courage, faith, and devotion to God. As a shepherd, David bravely defended his flock from predators, foreshadowing his future role as the shepherd king of Israel. David's faith was evident in his willingness to trust God in the face of overwhelming odds, such as his victory over Goliath the giant. However, David also had his flaws, including his tendency towards impulsivity and moral failure. His affair with Bathsheba and subsequent murder of her husband Uriah serve as a stark reminder of the consequences of sin.

Despite his many virtues, David sometimes acted impulsively and made rash decisions without considering the consequences. For example, when faced with the news of Nabal's refusal to provide assistance to his men, David reacted in anger and nearly slaughtered Nabal and his household before being restrained by Abigail's intervention (1 Samuel 25:1-38). This incident reveals David's propensity towards impulsive behavior and the need for wisdom and self-control.

The most infamous failure in David's life is his affair with Bathsheba and the subsequent murder of her husband Uriah. Despite being a man after God's own heart, David succumbed to temptation and committed adultery with Bathsheba, leading to a series of tragic consequences, including the death of their child and turmoil within David's own household (2 Samuel 11:1-27). This moral failure serves as a sobering reminder of the destructive power of sin and the importance of remaining vigilant against its allure.

As king, David struggled to maintain order within his own household and failed to discipline his children effectively. This laxity led to rebellion and strife within David's family, culminating in Absalom's rebellion and attempted coup against his father's throne (2 Samuel 15:1-12). David's failure to address these issues promptly and decisively contributed to the breakdown of his family and the stability of his kingdom.

God's Redemption Through David's Repentance:

Despite his flaws and moral failings, David remained a man after God's own heart, characterized by his genuine repentance and humility before God. When confronted by the prophet Nathan about his sins with Bathsheba and Uriah, David immediately acknowledged his guilt and repented before God (2 Samuel 12:1-14). His heartfelt prayer of confession and repentance in Psalm 51 serves as a poignant reminder of David's contrition and desire for restoration with God.

Conclusion:

David's life serves as a powerful reminder of the transformative power of repentance and God's grace. Despite his flaws and moral failings, David remained a man after God's own heart, characterized by his genuine repentance and humility before God. His willingness to acknowledge his sins and seek forgiveness serves as a model for all who seek to follow God faithfully.

One of the most striking aspects of David's story is the depth of his relationship with God. Despite his failures and shortcomings, David never lost sight of his dependence on God's mercy and grace. His heartfelt prayers of confession and repentance, as recorded in the Psalms, reflect David's deep desire for reconciliation and restoration with God. David's example challenges us to examine our own hearts and lives before God, acknowledging our sins and seeking His forgiveness and grace.

David's relationship with God also serves as a reminder of the importance of cultivating a vibrant and intimate connection with our Creator. Throughout his life, David sought after God with sincerity and devotion, pouring out his heart in prayer and worship. His Psalms are filled with expressions of praise, thanksgiving, and adoration, reflecting David's deep love for God and his desire to draw near to Him. David's example challenges us to prioritize our relationship with God above all else, seeking His presence and guidance in every area of our lives.

David's story is much more involved than this and well worth reading. He trusted God when things were bad, was patient waiting on God, waited on God to become king and faced many trials before he reached the throne. God uses all of our life experiences to develop trust in Him. David devoted his life to God and trusted in Him in all circumstances. I pray we can do the same.

David's life is a story of triumph and tragedy, victory and failure. Despite his flaws and moral failings, David remained a man after God's own heart, characterized by his faith, repentance, and humility before God. As we reflect on David's story, may we be challenged to examine our own hearts and lives before God. May we, like David, strive to remain faithful to God's call, trusting in His grace and forgiveness to redeem and restore us.

Reflective Questions - Answer in Writing

1. In what ways do David's strengths and weaknesses resonate with your own experiences and struggles?

2. Reflect on a time when you acted impulsively or made a rash decision. What were the consequences, and how did you learn from that experience?

3. Consider David's moral failure with Bathsheba and Uriah. How can we guard against similar temptations in our own lives?

4. Despite his flaws, David remained a man after God's own heart. How does his story give you hope for your own journey of faith and repentance?

5. How can you cultivate a spirit of humility and repentance, like David, in your own relationship with God?

Week 21: Philippian Jailer: From Cruelty to Compassion

The Philippian jailer, a person encountered in the book of Acts, provides a compelling narrative of transformation from cruelty to compassion through a powerful encounter with God. His story serves as a testament to the redemptive power of grace and the transformative impact of encountering the living God. In this lesson, we will delve into the Philippian jailer, examining his strengths, weaknesses, and the implications of his encounter with God for his own life.

Verse to Review: Acts 16:30-31

"He then brought them out and asked, 'Sirs, what must I do to be saved?' They replied, 'Believe in the Lord Jesus, and you will be saved—you and your household.'"

Background of the Philippian Jailer:

The Philippian jailer was tasked with overseeing the incarceration of Paul and Silas in Philippi, a Roman colony in Macedonia. As a representative of Roman authority, he likely operated within a system that prioritized control and punishment. However, his encounter with Paul and Silas amidst a supernatural earthquake would challenge his assumptions and lead to a radical transformation of his heart and life.

Strengths and Flaws of the Philippian Jailer:

Some of his strengths include:

1. **Commitment to Duty:** As a jailer, the Philippian jailer was likely diligent and committed to his duties, ensuring the security and order of the prison. His sense of responsibility and loyalty to his role reflect his integrity and work ethic. When he saw the prison doors were open, his immediate reaction was to grab his sword and take his own life.
2. **Recognition of Authority:** When confronted with the supernatural events surrounding Paul and Silas' imprisonment, the Philippian jailer recognized the authority and power of God at work. His acknowledgment of divine intervention set the stage for his willingness to seek salvation and surrender to God's sovereignty. He realized something different about Paul and wanted it!
3. **Desire for Salvation:** Despite his occupation and societal status, the Philippian jailer demonstrated a sincere hunger for spiritual truth and salvation. His question to Paul and Silas— "What must I do to be saved?"—revealed a heart open to the message of hope and redemption.

Some of his weaknesses include:

1. **Cruelty and Harshness:** As a jailer operating within the Roman system of law and order, the Philippian jailer likely engaged in practices that were harsh and punitive. His treatment of prisoners may have been characterized by cruelty and indifference to their suffering.

2. **Worldly Perspective:** Before his encounter with Paul and Silas, the Philippian jailer likely viewed the world through a lens shaped by Roman authority and societal norms. His understanding of power and control would have been influenced by worldly values rather than the principles of compassion and mercy.

3. **Ignorance of God's Grace:** Prior to encountering Paul and Silas, the Philippian jailer was ignorant of the message of God's grace and the possibility of salvation through faith in Jesus Christ. His spiritual blindness prevented him from experiencing the fullness of God's love and forgiveness.

God's Response to the Philippian Jailer:

Despite the Philippian jailer's past of cruelty and indifference, God responded to his sincere seeking after salvation with grace and mercy. Through the witness of Paul and Silas and the power of the Holy Spirit, the Philippian jailer experienced a radical transformation of heart and mind, leading to his conversion and baptism along with his household.

The story of the Philippian jailer serves as a powerful testimony to the transformative power of encountering God's grace and mercy. His journey from cruelty to compassion reflects the redemptive work of God in the lives of all who humbly seek Him and surrender to His will. Please fully read Acts 16:25-40.

Conclusion:

The Philippian jailer's story challenges us to reexamine our own attitudes and assumptions about power, authority, and justice. His encounter with Paul and Silas forced him to confront the cruelty and harshness of his own actions, leading to a profound transformation of his heart and perspective. In a world marked by injustice and oppression, the Philippian jailer's story serves as a powerful reminder of the transformative power of encountering God's grace and mercy, and the possibility of redemption for all who humble themselves before Him.

Moreover, the Philippian jailer's story highlights the importance of genuine repentance and faith in the process of spiritual transformation. His question to Paul and Silas—"What must I do to be saved?"—revealed an open heart to the message of hope and redemption and a willingness to surrender to God's will. As believers, we are called to follow the Philippian jailer's example, seeking after God with sincerity and humility, and trusting in His grace and mercy for our own lives. Take a minute and imagine the role reversal, the jailer went from a position of pure power, to complete loss of control when he woke up to doors open to asking how he can be saved, to being baptized!

This also underscores the significance of personal testimony and witness in the spread of the gospel. His encounter with God and his subsequent conversion had a ripple effect that impacted not only his own life but also the lives of those around him, including his household and the early Christian community. As believers, we are called to bear witness to the transformative power of Jesus Christ in our own lives, and to share the good news of salvation with others, regardless of their background or circumstances.

His story challenges us to reexamine our own attitudes and assumptions about power, authority, and justice, and to seek after God with sincerity and humility. His strengths and weaknesses serve as a reminder that no one is beyond the reach of God's love and forgiveness, and that genuine repentance and faith can lead to radical transformation.

Reflective Questions - Answer in Writing

1. In what ways do you see yourself in the strengths and weaknesses of the Philippian jailer?

2. Have you ever witnessed something that had to be God? Explain

3. Consider the barriers and prejudices that may exist in your own heart and worldview. How can you cultivate a spirit of compassion and mercy, following the example of the Philippian jailer?

4. Reflect on the transformative power of encountering God's grace in the Philippian jailer's life. How has your own encounter with God's grace impacted those around you?

5. How does the story of the Philippian jailer challenge you to seek after God with sincerity and humility, trusting in His grace and mercy for your own life? Has God used your situations to show his love? Are you listening?

Week 22: Jacob: Wrestling with God

Jacob, the grandson of Abraham, is a significant figure in the Bible, known for his complex character, his struggles, and his eventual transformation through encountering God. His life is marked by moments of deceit, conflict, and wrestling with both human and divine forces. In this lesson, we will explore the life of Jacob, examining his strengths, weaknesses, and the transformative power of encountering God.

Verse to Review: Genesis 32:28

"Then the man said, 'Your name will no longer be Jacob, but Israel, because you have struggled with God and with humans and have overcome.'"

Background of Jacob:

Jacob was the son of Isaac and Rebekah, and the younger twin brother of Esau. From birth, Jacob's life was marked by rivalry and conflict with his brother, culminating in his deception of Esau to obtain his birthright and blessing. Fleeing from Esau's wrath, Jacob encountered God at Bethel and received a vision of a ladder reaching into heaven, symbolizing God's presence and promise to bless him.

Strengths and Flaws of Jacob:

Jacob's life was filled with both strengths and weaknesses, some of his strengths include:

1. **Determination to Succeed:** Jacob was a determined person, willing to seize opportunities and overcome obstacles to achieve his goals. This could also be listed as a fault but of course is determined on a case by case basis.
2. **Faithfulness to God's Promises:** Despite his flaws, Jacob remained faithful to God's promises and sought His guidance and protection in times of trouble. He acknowledged God as the God of his father Isaac and the God of Abraham, demonstrating his commitment to the covenantal relationship with God. It is important that we depend on God in the good and bad times.
3. **Capacity for Transformation:** Jacob's encounter with God at Peniel, where he wrestled with a divine being until daybreak, resulted in a profound transformation. He emerged from the struggle with a new name, Israel. Jacob wrestled with God to secure the blessing that was meant for him since the beginning.

Weaknesses:

1. **Deceitfulness and Manipulation:** Throughout his life, Jacob resorted to deceit and manipulation to achieve his objectives, often at the expense of others. His deception of Esau and Laban, as well as his favoritism towards Joseph, resulted in familial discord and estrangement.
2. **Fear and Anxiety:** Jacob often struggled with fear and anxiety, especially when faced with uncertain circumstances or the threat of danger. His fear of Esau's retaliation led him to devise

elaborate schemes to protect himself and his family, rather than trusting in God's provision and protection. **Read Genesis 32:22-32**.

3. **Strife and Conflict:** Jacob's life was characterized by strife and conflict, both within his family and with external adversaries. His rivalry with Esau, his contentious relationship with Laban, and the jealousy and enmity among his sons contributed to a legacy of discord and division.

God's Redemption Through Jacob's Wrestling:

Despite his flaws and struggles, God remained faithful to Jacob and used his wrestling with God as a means of transformation and blessing. Through his encounter with God at Peniel, Jacob experienced a profound revelation of God's presence and power, which resulted in a new identity and purpose as Israel, the one who struggles with God.

Jacob's journey from deception and conflict to transformation and blessing serves as a powerful testimony to God's faithfulness and redemptive work in the lives of His people. Despite Jacob's shortcomings and struggles, God remained faithful to His promises and used Jacob's experiences to shape him into a vessel of His grace and blessing. **Think about a specific situation that God has done the same for you.**

Jacob's encounter with God at Peniel was a turning point in his life, marking the beginning of a new chapter characterized by surrender, humility, and faith. In wrestling with God, Jacob wrestled with his own identity and purpose, ultimately emerging with a new name and a renewed sense of calling. His transformation from Jacob, the deceiver, to Israel, the one who struggles with God, reflects the transformative power of encountering God's presence and grace.

Conclusion:

Jacob's life serves as a powerful reminder of God's faithfulness and redemptive work in the lives of His people. Despite Jacob's flaws and shortcomings, God remained faithful to His promises and used Jacob's experiences to shape him into a vessel of His grace and blessing. We are reminded of God's ability to redeem even the most broken and flawed and use them for His glory.

One of the most profound aspects of Jacob's journey is his encounter with God at Peniel, where he wrestled with a divine being until daybreak. This encounter symbolizes Jacob's struggle with his own identity and purpose, as well as his wrestling with God's will for his life. In wrestling with God, Jacob grappled with his past mistakes and struggles, ultimately emerging with a new name and a renewed sense of calling.

Jacob's journey also highlights the importance of surrender and humility in the process of transformation. Despite his resourcefulness and determination, Jacob ultimately had to surrender to God's will and acknowledge his own limitations. We cannot do this alone! It was in his surrender to God that Jacob found true fulfillment and blessing, as evidenced by his encounter with God and the subsequent reconciliation with Esau.

Like Jacob, we are all flawed and imperfect, yet God remains faithful to His promises and is able to transform our struggles into blessings for His glory. God remained faithful to him, using his experiences to shape him into a vessel of His grace and blessing. And may we trust in God's promises and providence, knowing that He is able to turn our struggles into blessings for His glory.

Reflective Questions - Answer in Writing

1. In what ways do you relate to Jacob's strengths and weaknesses?

2. Reflect on a time when you experienced a struggle or conflict in your faith journey. How did God work through that experience to bring about transformation and blessing?

3. Consider Jacob's capacity for resourcefulness and determination. How can we use our talents and abilities to serve God and others?

4. Reflect on Jacob's encounter with God at Peniel. How can we cultivate a similar openness to God's presence and guidance in our own lives?

5. How does Jacob's journey of wrestling with God and receiving blessing inspire you to trust in God's faithfulness and providence in your own life? Anything specifically stand out to you?

1 John 3:16 summarizes the essence of Christian love and sacrifice. It calls believers to love one another just as Christ loved us and laid down His life for us. This study will explore the context, meaning, and application of this verse, helping us understand the depth of Christ's love and how we are called to emulate it in our relationships with others.

The Book of 1 John

The First Epistle of John is a letter written by the Apostle John, addressing the early Christian community. The letter emphasizes themes such as love, fellowship with God, the nature of Christ, and ethical conduct. John writes to reassure believers of their faith and to encourage them to live out the love they have received from Christ.

Immediate Context

1 John 3:16 is situated within a passage where John discusses the nature of love and the evidence of being a child of God. In the preceding verses, John contrasts the behavior of those who live in darkness with those who walk in the light, emphasizing that true children of God practice righteousness and love one another.

Exploring 1 John 3:16

The Text

"This is how we know what love is: Jesus Christ laid down his life for us. And we ought to lay down our lives for our brothers and sisters" (1 John 3:16, NIV).

Key Phrases

1. **"This is how we know what love is"**

   o John introduces the ultimate example of love. Understanding true love begins with recognizing the sacrificial act of Jesus Christ.

2. **"Jesus Christ laid down his life for us"**

   o Jesus' sacrificial death on the cross is the definitive demonstration of love. His willingness to give His life for humanity is the highest expression of selfless love.

3. **"And we ought to lay down our lives for our brothers and sisters"**

   o Believers are called to emulate Christ's sacrificial love. This means being willing to make significant sacrifices for the well-being of others, putting their needs above our own.

Theological Implications

The Definition of Love

1 John 3:16 provides a clear and tangible definition of love. Love is not merely an emotion or a feeling but is demonstrated through self-sacrificial actions, mirroring Christ's love for us.

The Example of Christ

Jesus Christ serves as the ultimate example of love. His life and sacrificial death are the standard by which believers are to measure and practice love. Christ's love is active, selfless, and sacrificial.

The Call to Sacrifice

Believers are called to a high standard of love that involves self-sacrifice. This may not always mean physical death, but it does involve putting others' needs and well-being above our own comfort and desires.

Practical Applications

Demonstrating Sacrificial Love

Believers are called to actively seek ways to demonstrate sacrificial love in their daily lives. This can include acts of service, generosity, and putting others' needs before our own.

Building a Loving Community

A Christian community should be characterized by mutual love and support. This involves being attentive to the needs of others, offering help and encouragement, and fostering an environment where everyone feels valued and cared for.

Reflecting on Christ's Sacrifice

Regular reflection on Christ's sacrificial love can inspire and motivate believers to love others more deeply. This can be done through prayer, meditation on Scripture, and participating in the Lord's Supper.

Misunderstandings and Cautions

Misinterpreting Sacrifice

Sacrificial love does not mean neglecting self-care or enabling harmful behavior. True love seeks the well-being of others in a healthy and balanced manner, respecting boundaries and promoting mutual respect.

Overlooking Daily Acts of Love

While laying down one's life can seem like a grand gesture, sacrificial love is also expressed in everyday actions. Small acts of kindness, patience, and generosity are significant ways to embody Christ's love.

Avoiding Legalism

Practicing sacrificial love should not be reduced to a checklist of duties. It should flow naturally from a heart transformed by Christ's love and empowered by the Holy Spirit.

Biblical Examples

The Good Samaritan

The parable of the Good Samaritan (Luke 10:25-37) illustrates sacrificial love. The Samaritan goes out of his way to help a wounded stranger, providing care and resources despite cultural barriers and personal inconvenience.

Ruth and Naomi

The story of Ruth and Naomi (Ruth 1-4) demonstrates loyal and sacrificial love. Ruth's decision to stay with her mother-in-law, Naomi, and care for her despite the difficulties they faced is a powerful example of selfless devotion.

Jesus Washing the Disciples' Feet

In John 13:1-17, Jesus washes His disciples' feet, demonstrating humble service and sacrificial love. This act teaches that true love involves serving others, even in tasks that seem menial or uncomfortable.

Conclusion

1 John 3:16 calls believers to a profound and active love that mirrors the sacrificial love of Christ. As Christians, we are encouraged to look to Jesus as our ultimate example and to let His love inspire our actions. Through sacrificial love, we can build strong, supportive communities and reflect God's love to the world. By doing so, we honor Christ's sacrifice and fulfill our calling to be His disciples.

Reflective Questions – Answer in Writing

1. How do you currently demonstrate sacrificial love in your daily life, and in what areas can you grow?

2. What are some practical ways you can put others' needs before your own in your family, community, or church?

3. How does reflecting on Christ's sacrifice inspire and motivate you to love others more deeply?

4. Are there specific relationships or situations in your life where you find it challenging to practice sacrificial love? How can you seek God's help in these areas?

5. How can your Christian community better embody the principles of sacrificial love outlined in 1 John 3:16? What steps can you take to contribute to this goal?

Week 24: Cornelius: A Gentile's Journey to Faith

Cornelius, a Roman centurion, is an often-overlooked figure in the New Testament who played a significant role in the early spread of Christianity. His story, recorded in the book of Acts, serves as a powerful testimony to God's inclusive love and the transformative power of faith. In this lesson, we will explore the life of Cornelius, examining his strengths, weaknesses, and the profound implications of his encounter with God for the expansion of the early Christian movement.

Verse to Review: Acts 10:1-2

"At Caesarea there was a man named Cornelius, a centurion in what was known as the Italian Regiment. He and all his family were devout and God-fearing; he gave generously to those in need and prayed to God regularly."

Background of Cornelius:

Cornelius was a Roman centurion stationed in Caesarea, a coastal city in Judea. Despite being a Gentile and an outsider to the Jewish faith, Cornelius was described as devout and God-fearing, demonstrating a sincere seeking after the one true God. He was known for his generosity towards those in need and his commitment to prayer and worship.

Strengths and Flaws of Cornelius:

Cornelius possessed both strengths and weaknesses that shaped his character and journey of faith. Some of his strengths include:

1. **Devotion and Piety:** Cornelius was characterized by his devoutness and reverence for God, evident in his regular prayers and acts of worship. His sincere seeking of God set him apart as a person desperately wanting genuine faith and spiritually hungry.
2. **Generosity and Compassion:** Cornelius demonstrated a compassionate heart and a willingness to help those in need, as seen in his generous giving to the poor and marginalized. His acts of charity showed a genuine concern for others and mirrored the compassion of God.
3. **Openness to Divine Guidance:** Despite being a Gentile, Cornelius remained open to the leading of God's Spirit and obediently followed the instructions he received in a vision to send for the apostle Peter. His willingness to heed divine guidance led to a significant encounter with God and the transformation of his life and household.

However, Cornelius also had his flaws and weaknesses:

1. **Limited Understanding of God's Revelation:** As a Gentile living in a predominantly pagan society, Cornelius likely had a limited understanding of God's revelation and the Jewish

scriptures. His knowledge of God was incomplete or distorted by cultural influences, leading to a sincere but imperfect faith.

2. **Cultural Barriers and Prejudices:** As a Roman centurion, Cornelius would have been accustomed to the cultural norms and prejudices of his time, including attitudes of superiority towards non-Roman cultures and religions. His encounter with Peter and the message of Jesus challenged his worldview and forced him to confront his own biases and preconceptions.

3. **Lack of Exposure:** Cornelius demonstrated exceptional devotion, steadfast in his worship of the one true God. However, even in his devoutness, he lacked exposure to the gospel's transformative message. Hence, God orchestrated Peter's mission to convey the pivotal narrative of Christ's crucifixion and resurrection to Cornelius (referenced in Acts 10:39–40, 43). It was only upon embracing the message of Jesus that Cornelius and his household encountered the profound influence of the Holy Spirit, marking their spiritual rebirth. The account of Cornelius not only underscores the essentiality of the gospel but also highlights divine intervention in ensuring its dissemination to those earnestly receptive.

God's Response to Cornelius:

Despite Cornelius' status as a Gentile and an outsider to the Jewish faith, God responded to his sincere seeking after truth and righteousness. Through a series of divine interventions, including visions and angelic visitations, God orchestrated a meeting between Cornelius and the apostle Peter, leading to Cornelius' conversion and the baptism of him and his household in the Holy Spirit.

The story of Cornelius serves as a powerful testament to God's inclusive love and His desire to reconcile all people to Himself. Cornelius' faithfulness and obedience to God's leading paved the way for the inclusion of Gentiles into the early Christian community, breaking down barriers of ethnicity, nationality, and social status. Are you seeking a personal relationship with Christ daily? Do you talk to Him daily? Try it out!

Conclusion:

Cornelius' story challenges us to reexamine our own attitudes and assumptions about faith, ethnicity, and social status. His encounter with Peter and the message of Jesus forced him to confront his own biases and prejudices, leading to a radical transformation of his worldview and his understanding of God's inclusive love. In a world marked by division and hostility, Cornelius' example serves as a powerful reminder of the transformative power of faith to break down barriers and build bridges of reconciliation and unity.

Moreover, Cornelius' story highlights the importance of divine encounter and guidance in the faith journey of believers. **Like Cornelius, we are called to remain open to the leading of God's Spirit and obedient to His voice, even when it leads us outside of our comfort zones or challenges our**

preconceived notions. God's ways are not our ways and His plans often transcend our understanding, requiring us to trust in His wisdom and goodness.

Furthermore, Cornelius' story underscores the significance of personal testimony and witness in the spread of the gospel. His encounter with God and his subsequent conversion had a ripple effect that impacted not only his own life but also the lives of those around him, including his household and the early Christian community. As believers, we are called to bear witness to the transformative power of Jesus Christ in our own lives and to share the good news of salvation with others, **regardless of their background or circumstances.**

Cornelius' life offers valuable lessons for believers today, reminding us of the universal scope of God's redemptive plan and the transformative power of faith. His strengths and weaknesses serve as a reminder that God looks not at outward appearances but at the heart and that sincere seeking after God will be met with His gracious response. It is also important to know that no matter where you came from, no matter who you were you are accepted in Christ.

Reflective Questions - Answer in Writing

1. In what ways do you see yourself in the strengths and weaknesses of Cornelius?

2. When you pray, you are talking to God directly. Praying does not just have to be with your eyes closed, name other times you have spent time dedicated to talking to our Creator?

3. Consider the barriers and prejudices that may exist in your own heart and worldview. How can you cultivate a spirit of openness and inclusivity, following Cornelius' example?

4. Reflect on the transformative power of faith in Cornelius' life and household. How has your own faith journey impacted those around you?

5. How does the story of Cornelius challenge you to step out in faith and obedience, trusting in God's leading and His inclusive love for all people?

Week 25: Samson: Finding Strength in Weakness

The story of Samson is one of both incredible strength and profound weakness. Despite his flaws and failures, Samson's life serves as a testament to God's ability to work through imperfect people to accomplish His purposes. In this lesson, we will dive into the life of Samson, exploring his strengths, weaknesses, and how God used him for His glory.

Verse to Review: Judges 13:5

"You will become pregnant and have a son whose head is never to be touched by a razor because the boy is to be a Nazirite, dedicated to God from the womb. He will take the lead in delivering Israel from the hands of the Philistines."

History of Samson:

Samson was born during a time of oppression for the Israelites under the rule of the Philistines. He was set apart by God as a Nazirite from birth, meaning he was dedicated to God and bound by specific vows, including abstaining from alcohol and avoiding contact with dead bodies (Judges 13:4-5). Samson's birth was announced by an angel of the Lord to his parents, who were previously barren, signifying his special role in delivering Israel from their enemies.

Samson's Strengths and Flaws:

Samson's most obvious strength was his physical ability, which he used to defeat the enemies of Israel, often single-handedly. His exploits included tearing apart a lion with his bare hands (Judges 14:5-6), killing thirty Philistines to settle a bet (Judges 14:19), and destroying a Philistine temple, killing thousands of enemies in his final act of defiance (Judges 16:28-30).

However, Samson's weaknesses were equally prominent. He struggled with self-control and a lack of judgement, particularly in his relationships with women. His infatuation with Delilah, a Philistine woman, ultimately led to his downfall, as he revealed the secret of his strength to her, resulting in his capture and enslavement by the Philistines (Judges 16:4-21).

God's Redemption Through Samson's Weakness:

Despite Samson's flaws and failures, God remained faithful to His promise to deliver Israel through him. In his lowest moment, imprisoned and blinded by the Philistines, Samson called upon God for strength one last time. In a display of divine power, God granted Samson supernatural strength, allowing him to bring down the temple of Dagon, killing himself and many Philistines in the process (Judges 16:28-30).

Conclusion:

Samson's life is woven with moments of triumph and tragedy, each revealing deeper truths about human nature and the character of God. From his miraculous birth to his final act of sacrifice, Samson's story captivates our imagination and challenges our understanding of divine providence.

One of the most intriguing aspects of Samson's story is the tension between his extraordinary strength and his glaring weaknesses. On the one hand, Samson's physical strength was unmatched, allowing him to perform feats of strength that defied human capability. Yet, beneath this outward veneer of strength lay a man plagued by moral frailty and impulsive behavior. We all have strengths and weaknesses.

Samson's weakness for women is a recurring theme throughout his narrative, leading him into dangerous associations that ultimately brought about his downfall. His ill-fated relationship with Delilah, in particular, serves as a cautionary tale about the consequences of succumbing to temptation and forsaking one's calling. Despite several warnings, Samson's infatuation with Delilah blinded him to the perilous path he was treading, ultimately leading to his capture and humiliation at the hands of his enemies.

Yet, even in his darkest hour, Samson's story is not devoid of redemption. In the depths of his despair, imprisoned and shorn of his strength, Samson's faith in God is rekindled, leading to a final act of sacrificial heroism that secures his place among the heroes of Israel. In his death, Samson achieves a victory far greater than any he accomplished in life, striking a decisive blow against the enemies of God's people and inspiring future generations with his example of faithfulness and courage.

Samson's story challenges us to confront our own weaknesses and shortcomings, reminding us that even the strongest among us are vulnerable to the snares of sin and temptation. Yet, it also offers hope, reminding us that God's grace is greater than our failings and that He can use even the most flawed and imperfect vessels to accomplish His purposes.

As we reflect on Samson's life, may we be inspired to emulate his faithfulness and courage, even in the face of overwhelming odds. May we also be reminded of the boundless grace of our heavenly Father, who stands ready to forgive and restore us when we fumble. And may we, like Samson, find strength in weakness, trusting in the power of God to accomplish His purposes through us, despite our flaws and failings. Your mistakes in the past can be used to glorify God.

Samson's life is complex, of strength, weakness, and redemption. Despite his flaws, God used Samson to accomplish His purposes and deliver His people from oppression. As we reflect on Samson's story, may we be reminded that God can use even our weaknesses for His glory. Let us strive to find strength in Him, knowing that His power is made perfect in our weakness.

Reflective Questions - Answer in Writing

1. In what areas of your life do you struggle with self-control or lack discernment, like Samson did?

2. Reflect on a time when you experienced God's strength in your weakness. How did that experience impact your faith?

3. Consider the consequences of Samson's actions, particularly in his relationship with Delilah. How can we learn from his mistakes in our own relationships?

4. Despite his flaws, God still used Samson to accomplish His purposes. How does this give you hope for your own life, despite your imperfections?

5. How can you rely more on God's strength and less on your own abilities in your daily life?

Week 26: Matthew 25:40 - Serving Others as Serving Christ

Matthew 25:40 is a powerful verse that captures the essence of Christian service and ministry. In this verse, Jesus teaches that whatever we do for the least of His brothers and sisters, we do for Him. This profound truth challenges believers to recognize the presence of Christ in the marginalized, oppressed, and needy, and to respond with compassion, mercy, and love. We will explore the significance of Matthew 25:40, reflecting on its implications for our lives and our call to serve others as serving Christ Himself.

Matthew 25:40

"The King will reply, 'Truly I tell you, whatever you did for one of the least of these brothers and sisters of mine, you did for me.'"

Understanding Matthew 25:40:

Matthew 25:40 is part of Jesus' teaching on the final judgment, commonly referred to as the "parable of the sheep and the goats." In this parable, Jesus describes how the King (representing Himself) will separate the righteous from the unrighteous based on their actions towards the least of His brothers and sisters. Those who cared for the hungry, thirsty, stranger, naked, sick, and imprisoned are commended and invited into the kingdom of heaven, while those who neglected to do so are condemned.

Key Themes in Matthew 25:40:

1. **Identification with Christ:** Jesus identifies Himself with the marginalized and vulnerable members of society, emphasizing the intimate connection between serving others and serving Him. This challenges believers to view every act of service as an opportunity to encounter and minister – to show compassion and mercy for the least of these.
2. **Compassion and Empathy:** Matthew 25:40 underscores the importance of compassion and empathy towards those in need. By caring for the least of His brothers and sisters, believers demonstrate their love for Christ and fulfill the command to love their neighbors as themselves. Have you practiced this in the last week? What could you do differently?
3. **Social Justice and Mercy:** Jesus' teaching in Matthew 25:40 highlights the **biblical mandate** for social justice and mercy. Christians are called to advocate for the rights and dignity of the oppressed, provide for the needs of the marginalized and extend mercy and compassion to those who are suffering. This is true for you now and 10 years from now.
4. **Eternal Consequences:** The final judgment described in Matthew 25:40 emphasizes the eternal consequences of our actions towards others. Believers are reminded that their treatment of the least of His brothers and sisters has implications for their standing in the kingdom of heaven.

Brand 316 Inc www.brand316.org 727 North Waco #290 Wichita KS 67203 (316) 247-2050

Practical Application of Matthew 25:40:

1. **Recognizing Christ in Others:** Believers are called to develop spiritual warmth to recognize the presence of Christ in the marginalized, oppressed, and needy. This requires humility, empathy, and a willingness to engage with those who are often overlooked or ignored by society.
2. **Acting with Compassion:** Matthew 25:40 challenges Christians to respond to the needs of others with compassion, mercy, and love. This may involve acts of service such as feeding the hungry, clothing the naked, visiting the sick and imprisoned and welcoming strangers.
3. **Advocating for Justice:** We are called to advocate for justice and righteousness in their communities, standing up for the rights and dignity of the oppressed. This can involve speaking out against injustice, supporting organizations and initiatives that promote social justice, volunteering to help others and actively working towards systemic change.
4. **Living with Eternal Perspective:** Matthew 25:40 reminds believers of the eternal significance of their actions towards others. By investing in kingdom-focused activities and prioritizing the needs of the least of us we are following Christ's commands!

Conclusion:

Matthew 25:40 challenges Christians to review their priorities and values in light of the kingdom of God. This profound truth calls us to shift our focus from self-centeredness to other-centeredness, from material increase to spiritual investment, and from worldly pursuits to eternal significance. By recognizing Christ in the marginalized, oppressed, and needy, we participate in God's redemptive work in the world and bear witness to the transformative power of the gospel.

Moreover, it underscores the importance of cultivating a heart of compassion, empathy, and love towards others. As followers of Christ, we are called to embody the love of God in our interactions and relationships with those around us, extending grace, mercy, and kindness to all. This requires a willingness to step outside of our comfort zones, engage with diverse perspectives and experiences, and actively seek opportunities to serve and minister to others in practical ways.

It also challenges believers to advocate for justice and decency in their communities. The biblical mandate for social justice compels us to speak out against oppression, inequality, and systemic injustice, and to work towards creating a world where all people are treated with dignity, respect, and equality.

In conclusion, Matthew 25:40 is a powerful reminder of the intimate connection between serving others and serving Christ Himself. As we reflect on this, may we be inspired to live lives of compassion, mercy, and love towards our brothers and sisters, recognizing the eternal significance of our actions in the kingdom of God. May we also be challenged to advocate for justice and righteousness in our communities, standing up for the rights and dignity of the marginalized and oppressed, and working towards creating a world where God's kingdom values of love, justice, and peace are fully realized.

Reflective Questions - Answer in Writing

1. How does Matthew 25:40 challenge your understanding of Christian service and ministry?

2. Reflect on a time when you encountered Christ in the marginalized or oppressed. How did this experience impact your perspective on serving others?

3. How can you actively respond to the needs of the least of these that we all see daily?

4. Reflect on the eternal consequences described in Matthew 25:40. How does this influence your priorities and values in life?

5. In what ways can you incorporate these principles into your daily interactions and relationships with others?

Week 27: Gideon: Farmer to Warrior to Judge

Gideon, a judge and military leader in ancient Israel, is celebrated for his remarkable transformation from a timid farmer to a valiant warrior. His story illustrates God's power to use unlikely people for His purposes and the importance of faith and obedience in fulfilling God's calling. It is important to understand this theme – God can use you no matter your past. He loves you and cares about you. In this lesson, we will explore the life of Gideon, examining his strengths, weaknesses, and the transformative power of God's presence in his life.

Verse to Review: Judges 6:12

"When the angel of the Lord appeared to Gideon, he said, 'The Lord is with you, mighty warrior.'"

Background of Gideon:

Gideon lived during a tumultuous period in Israel's history, characterized by oppression and invasion by the Midianites. Despite his humble origins as a member of the weakest clan in Manasseh, Gideon was chosen by God to deliver Israel from the hands of their oppressors. Initially hesitant and insecure, Gideon's encounter with God's angelic messenger set him on a path of courage and leadership.

Strengths and Flaws of Gideon:

Strengths

1. **Humility and Dependence:** Gideon displayed humility and dependence on God, acknowledging his own inadequacy and weakness. He recognized the need for divine intervention and guidance in the face of overwhelming odds. We all need to live a life dependent on Him.
2. **Courage and Leadership:** Despite his initial reluctance, Gideon demonstrated courage and leadership in rallying the Israelite troops against the Midianites. He inspired confidence and unity among his fellow Israelites, leading them into battle with faith and determination.
3. **Strategic Thinking:** Gideon exhibited strategic thinking and creativity in planning and executing his military strategies. His unconventional tactics, such as the use of trumpets, torches, and clay jars, proved instrumental in achieving victory over the Midianite army.

Weaknesses

1. **Doubt and Insecurity:** Gideon struggled with doubt and insecurity, questioning God's presence and power in his life. He sought reassurance through signs and miracles, indicating a lack of confidence in God's promises. We are called to not test the Lord!
2. **Fear of Failure:** Gideon's fear of failure and the potential consequences of his actions often hindered his willingness to step out in faith. He hesitated to confront the Midianites and required multiple confirmations from God before taking decisive action. It is common to fear failure but understand with your faith in Christ; all things will work out for His Glory!

111

Brand 316 Inc www.brand316.org 727 North Waco #290 Wichita KS 67203 (316) 247-2050

3. **Idolatry and Compromise:** Despite his initial commitment to God, Gideon later succumbed to idolatry and compromise, erecting an ephod as a symbol of his victory and receiving tribute from his people. His actions compromised his integrity and led to spiritual decline.

God's Redemption Through Gideon's Weakness:

Despite his flaws and weaknesses, God used Gideon as a vessel for His glory and a catalyst for Israel's deliverance from oppression. Through Gideon's obedience and reliance on God, the Israelites experienced a miraculous victory over the Midianites, affirming God's power to accomplish His purposes through frail and imperfect individuals.

Gideon's encounter with God's angelic messenger marked a turning point in his life. Despite his doubts and insecurities, Gideon received a divine commission and assurance of God's presence and power with him. The transformation from a fearful farmer hiding from the Midianites to a courageous leader rallying Israel to battle illustrates the profound impact of encountering God's presence and promises.

Conclusion:

Gideon's story not only serves as a testament to God's faithfulness and power but also offers valuable insights into the nature of faith and obedience. Despite his initial doubts and insecurities, Gideon ultimately embraced God's calling and stepped into his role as a leader and deliverer of Israel. His journey from weakness to strength is a powerful reminder that God often chooses the least likely candidates to accomplish His purposes, demonstrating His sovereignty and wisdom in selecting individuals who rely on Him for strength and guidance.

One of the most striking aspects of Gideon's story is his willingness to trust in God's promises and obey His commands, even when they seemed daunting or illogical. When God instructed Gideon to reduce the size of his army to a mere 300 men, Gideon could have easily doubted or questioned God's wisdom. Instead, he chose to obey without hesitation, confident that God would deliver Israel from their enemies. This radical obedience demonstrates Gideon's growing faith and reliance on God's power rather than his own strength or resources. **Are you willing to be radically obedient in Christ?**

Gideon's reliance on God's guidance and provision is further highlighted by his willingness to seek confirmation through signs and miracles. While some may view Gideon's requests for signs as evidence of his lack of faith, they can also be seen as expressions of humility and dependence on God's wisdom. Gideon's desire for assurance reflects his recognition of his own limitations and his trust in God's ability to confirm His will through miraculous interventions. **What are your specific thoughts about that?**

Gideon's story reminds us of the dangers of spiritual compromise and idolatry. Despite his initial victory over the Midianites and the miraculous signs he witnessed, Gideon later succumbed to the temptation to exalt himself and receive tribute from his people. His decision to fashion an ephod as a symbol of his victory and accept gold as tribute from the Israelites ultimately led to spiritual decline and division among the people. This serves as a sobering reminder that even the most faithful servants of God are susceptible to pride and spiritual compromise if they fail to remain humble and obedient to God's commands. How can you have checks and balances in place to ensure you do not fall into the same scenario? Mentorship is one simple answer but come up with several options for yourself.

Despite his flaws and shortcomings, Gideon's unwavering trust in God's promises and his willingness to obey His commands set him apart as a mighty warrior and leader of Israel. As we reflect on Gideon's story, may we be inspired to trust in God's power to transform our weaknesses into strengths and to obey His commands with courage and faith, knowing that He is faithful to accomplish His purposes through us.

Reflective Questions - Answer in Writing

1. In what ways do you relate to Gideon's strengths and weaknesses?

2. Reflect on a time when you felt inadequate or insecure in fulfilling God's calling. How did God provide strength and assurance in that situation?

3. Consider Gideon's dependence on God for guidance and direction. How can we create a similar reliance on God's wisdom and provision in our own lives?

4. Reflect on Gideon's courage and leadership in the face of adversity. How can we overcome our fears and insecurities to step out in faith and obedience?

5. How does Gideon's story inspire you to trust in God's power to transform weakness into strength and accomplish His purposes through your life?

2 Thessalonians 3:16 is a powerful verse about the promise of peace from the Lord in all circumstances. That does not mean in some circumstances, but all circumstances. This study will help us understand how we can experience the peace of Christ in our daily lives and extend it to others. This is possible in the best and worst of times and no matter your specific situation. God is with you!

The Book of 2 Thessalonians

2 Thessalonians is a letter written by the Apostle Paul to the church in Thessalonica. The letter addresses concerns about the return of Christ, the need for steadfastness in faith, and instructions for orderly living within the Christian community. Paul emphasizes hope, encouragement, and perseverance in the face of trials.

Immediate Context

In 2 Thessalonians 3, Paul provides practical instructions for living, warns against idleness, and encourages the believers to continue doing good. Verse 16 serves as a benediction, a closing prayer of peace and blessing for the believers.

Exploring 2 Thessalonians 3:16

The Text

"Now may the Lord of peace himself give you peace at all times and in every way. The Lord be with all of you." (2 Thessalonians 3:16, NIV)

Key Phrases

1. **"The Lord of peace himself"**

   o   This title emphasizes that Jesus is the source and giver of true peace. He embodies peace and has the authority to bestow it upon His followers.

2. **"Give you peace at all times and in every way"**

   o   This phrase underscores the comprehensive and constant nature of the peace that Christ offers. It is available in all circumstances and situations.

3. **"The Lord be with all of you"**

   o   This is a reminder of Christ's abiding presence with believers, assuring them of His continual companionship and support.

<h1 style="text-align:center">Theological Implications</h1>

The Source of Peace

Paul identifies Jesus as the "Lord of peace," highlighting that true peace comes from Him. This peace is not dependent on external circumstances but is rooted in the presence and promises of Christ.

The Promise of Constant Peace

The peace that Jesus offers is available **"at all times and in every way."** This means that regardless of the situation—whether in times of joy or hardship, calm or chaos—Christians can experience His peace. This peace transcends understanding and guards the hearts and minds of believers.

The Presence of Christ

The assurance that "the Lord be with all of you" emphasizes the continual presence of Christ with His followers. His presence brings comfort, strength, and peace, enabling believers to face any challenge with confidence.

<h1 style="text-align:center">Practical Applications</h1>

Seeking the Lord of Peace

- **Prayer**: Regularly pray for the peace of Christ to fill your heart and mind. Invite Him into your daily life and circumstances.

- **Scripture**: Meditate on Bible verses about peace and allow God's Word to speak to your heart and renew your mind.

Embracing Peace in All Circumstances

- **Trusting God**: Trust in God's sovereignty and goodness, even when situations are difficult. Remember that His peace is not based on circumstances but on His unchanging nature.

- **Practicing Gratitude**: Develop a habit of gratitude, focusing on God's blessings and faithfulness. Gratitude can shift your perspective and help you experience peace.

Extending Peace to Others

- **Peacemaking**: Actively seek to promote peace in your relationships and community. Resolve conflicts with grace and strive to be a peacemaker.

- **Encouragement**: Encourage others with the message of Christ's peace. Share testimonies of how His peace has impacted your life and offer support to those who are struggling.

<h1 style="text-align:center">Misunderstandings and Cautions</h1>

Misunderstanding Peace as Absence of Conflict

Peace in Christ does not mean the absence of conflict or difficulties. It is the presence of His calm and assurance in the midst of challenges. Be cautious about equating peace with a trouble-free life.

Overlooking the Need for Active Trust

Experiencing the peace of Christ requires active trust and reliance on Him. It is not a passive state but involves continually turning to Him in faith and dependence.

Biblical Examples

Jesus Calming the Storm

In Mark 4:35-41, Jesus calms a storm, demonstrating His authority over nature and His ability to bring peace in the midst of chaos. The disciples' fear turns to awe as they witness His power and presence.

Paul and Silas in Prison

In Acts 16:16-40, Paul and Silas sing hymns and pray while imprisoned, displaying remarkable peace despite their circumstances. Their faith and peace lead to the conversion of the jailer and his household.

The Early Church

The early church faced persecution and hardships but continued to experience and spread the peace of Christ. Acts 9:31 describes the church as being "strengthened; and encouraged by the Holy Spirit, it grew in numbers, living in the fear of the Lord."

Conclusion

2 Thessalonians 3:16 offers a powerful promise of peace from the Lord of peace Himself. As Christians, we are called to seek and embrace the peace of Christ in all circumstances. Let us trust in His presence, rely on His promises, and actively promote peace in our relationships and communities.

Reflective Questions – Answer in Writing

1. How can you create a deeper experience of Christ's peace in your daily life?

2. In what situations do you find it most challenging to experience peace and how can you trust God more in those moments?

3. How can you actively promote peace in your relationships and community?

4. What practical steps can you take to remind yourself of Christ's presence with you?

5. How does understanding the comprehensive nature of Christ's peace impact your view of challenging circumstances?

117

Week 29: Miriam: The Sister of Moses and Aaron

Miriam, the sister of Moses and Aaron, is a prominent figure in the Old Testament narrative, known for her leadership among the Israelites and her role in the exodus from Egypt. Miriam's life is also marked by moments of weakness, particularly in her struggle with gossip and envy.

Verse to Review: Numbers 12:1-2

"Miriam and Aaron began to talk against Moses because of his Cushite wife, for he had married a Cushite. 'Has the Lord spoken only through Moses?' they asked. 'Hasn't he also spoken through us?' And the Lord heard this."

Background of Miriam:

Miriam was the older sister of Moses and Aaron, born to Amram and Jochebed during Israel's enslavement in Egypt. Miriam played a crucial role in the early life of Moses, watching over him as he was placed in a basket and set adrift in the Nile River to escape Pharaoh's decree to kill all Hebrew male infants. Miriam's quick thinking and resourcefulness led to Moses' rescue by Pharaoh's daughter, who adopted him as her own. After the miraculous deliverance of the Israelites from slavery in Egypt, Miriam led the women in a song of praise and celebration, known as the "Song of Miriam" (Exodus 15:20-21). Her leadership and spiritual insight were acknowledged by the Israelite community.

Strengths and Flaws of Miriam:

Some of her strengths include:

1. **Leadership and Courage:** Miriam demonstrated leadership and courage from a young age, boldly defying Pharaoh's decree to kill Hebrew male infants and helping to facilitate Moses' rescue and upbringing. Her bravery and determination played a crucial role in the preservation of Israel's future deliverer.
2. **Creativity and Resourcefulness:** Miriam exhibited creativity and resourcefulness in her leadership of the Israelite women, organizing them in joyful celebration and worship following the miraculous crossing of the Red Sea. Her ability to inspire and mobilize others contributed to the unity and cohesion of the Israelite community.
3. **Spiritual Sensitivity:** Miriam possessed a deep spiritual sensitivity and connection with God, as evidenced by her prophetic gifts and her role as a spokesperson for God among the Israelites. Her intimate relationship with God empowered her to speak truth to power and advocate for justice on behalf of her people.

Some of her weaknesses include:

1. **Jealousy and Resentment:** Miriam's most prominent weakness is evident in her role in criticizing Moses' leadership and questioning his authority. In Numbers 12:1-16, Miriam, along with Aaron, speaks against Moses, expressing jealousy or resentment toward him, particularly regarding his Cushite wife. This jealousy leads to God's rebuke of Miriam, resulting in her being afflicted with leprosy. Miriam's envy and resentment toward Moses highlight her susceptibility to feelings of rivalry and discontentment, which ultimately lead to her downfall.

2. **Pride and Self-Righteousness:** Another weakness displayed by Miriam is pride and self-righteousness, particularly in her assumption of authority or superiority over Moses. Miriam's challenge to Moses' leadership suggests a sense of self-importance or arrogance, as she and Aaron question Moses' credentials and criticize his decisions. This prideful attitude contributes to her disobedience and rebellion against God's appointed leader, highlighting her need for humility and submission to God's authority.

3. **Lack of Humility and Submission:** Miriam's failure to humble herself before God and submit to His appointed leadership through Moses resulted in her swift discipline and correction. Her refusal to acknowledge her wrongdoing and repent of her sin led to her temporary exclusion from the camp and a period of isolation and reflection.

4. **Failure to Accept Responsibility:** Following her punishment of leprosy, Miriam's response to her wrongdoing is not explicitly recorded in the biblical narrative. However, her silence in the aftermath of God's judgment suggests a potential reluctance or failure to accept responsibility for her actions. Instead of acknowledging her fault and seeking forgiveness, Miriam may have struggled with pride or stubbornness, hindering her ability to repent and reconcile with God and Moses. This failure to accept responsibility underscores the importance of humility and accountability in the process of repentance and restoration.

God's Response to Miriam:

God responded to her with both discipline and grace. He chastised her for her sinful behavior but also extended mercy and forgiveness, ultimately restoring her to fellowship with Him and her community. Miriam's encounter with God serves as a reminder of His holiness, justice, and compassion towards His people. The story of Miriam offers valuable lessons for believers today, reminding us of the dangers of gossip and envy and the importance of humility and submission to God's authority. Her strengths and weaknesses remind us about the destructive power of jealousy and resentment and the need for repentance and reconciliation with God and others.

Conclusion:

Miriam's story challenges us to confront the destructive power of gossip and envy in our own lives and communities. Her struggle with jealousy and resentment serves as a cautionary tale about the dangers of allowing sinful attitudes to take root in our hearts, leading to division, discord, and spiritual stagnation. As believers, we are called to guard our hearts against the subtle temptations of jealousy and envy, and to cultivate an attitude of gratitude and contentment in all circumstances.

Moreover, Miriam's story underscores the importance of humility and submission to God's authority. Her refusal to acknowledge Moses' unique role as God's chosen leader resulted in her swift discipline and correction, highlighting the consequences of pride and self-importance. As followers of Christ, we are called to humble ourselves before God and submit to His appointed leadership, trusting in His wisdom and guidance to direct our paths.

Furthermore, Miriam's story serves as a reminder of God's faithfulness and mercy towards His people, even in the midst of their sin and disobedience. Despite Miriam's failures, God responded to her with both discipline and grace, ultimately restoring her to fellowship with Him and her community. His response to Miriam's sin demonstrates His holiness, justice, and compassion, and His desire for repentance and reconciliation with His people.

Miriam's life presents a complex portrait of leadership, courage, and vulnerability to sin. Miriam's life offers valuable insights into the dangers of gossip and envy and the importance of humility and submission to God's authority. Her story challenges us to confront the sinful attitudes that threaten to undermine our relationships with God and others, and to cultivate a heart of gratitude, humility, and contentment. May we be inspired to guard our hearts against jealousy and resentment, and to embrace God's sovereignty and grace in our life.

Reflective Questions - Answer in Writing

1. In what ways do you see yourself in the strengths and weaknesses of Miriam?

2. Reflect on a time when you struggled with gossip or envy. How did this impact your relationships with others and your walk with God?

3. Consider the consequences of Miriam's gossip and envy on her own life and the community. How can you guard your heart against similar pitfalls?

4. Reflect on God's response to Miriam's sin, including His discipline and His grace. How does this demonstrate His character and His desire for repentance and restoration?

5. How does the story of Miriam challenge you to cultivate humility, submission, and gratitude in your own life, trusting in God's sovereignty and grace to lead you on the path of righteousness?

Philippians 4:7 speaks about the peace of God, which transcends all understanding. This verse encourages Christians to experience God's peace through prayer and thanksgiving, regardless of their circumstances. It is so important to understand and know that no matter your situation, how difficult it is or impossible it seems that God is with you.

The Book of Philippians

The Book of Philippians is a letter written by the Apostle Paul to the church in Philippi. Paul wrote this letter while he was imprisoned, yet it is filled with joy and encouragement. The letter emphasizes themes such as joy, unity, humility, and the peace that comes from trusting in God.

Immediate Context

Philippians 4:7 is part of Paul's advice to the Philippians in chapter 4, where he encourages them to rejoice in the Lord, be gentle, and not be anxious about anything. Instead, Paul instructs them to present their requests to God through prayer and petition with thanksgiving, promising that the peace of God will guard their hearts and minds.

Exploring Philippians 4:7

The Text

"And the peace of God, which transcends all understanding, will guard your hearts and your minds in Christ Jesus" (Philippians 4:7, NIV).

Key Phrases

1. **"The peace of God"**

   o This phrase refers to the calmness and peacefulness that comes from God. It is a divine peace that is not dependent on external circumstances.

2. **"Which transcends all understanding"**

   o God's peace surpasses human comprehension. It is beyond what we can fully grasp or explain, offering a sense of calm even in the midst of chaos and uncertainty.

3. **"Will guard your hearts and your minds"**

   o The peace of God acts as a protective barrier for our hearts (emotions) and minds (thoughts), safeguarding us from anxiety, fear, and worry.

4. **"In Christ Jesus"**

   o   This peace is found in a relationship with Christ. It is through our connection to Jesus that we experience and maintain this divine peace.

Theological Implications

The Source of Peace

Philippians 4:7 emphasizes that true peace comes from God. It is not something we can achieve on our own but is a gift from God that we receive through faith and prayer.

The Supernatural Nature of God's Peace

The verse highlights the supernatural aspect of God's peace. It transcends human understanding and logic, providing calmness and assurance even in difficult situations.

The Role of Prayer and Thanksgiving

Prayer and giving thanks to God are essential practices for experiencing God's peace. By presenting our requests to God and expressing gratitude, we open ourselves to receiving His peace.

Practical Applications

Cultivating a Prayerful Life

Regular prayer is crucial for experiencing God's peace. By developing a habit of bringing our concerns and requests to God, we can experience His calming presence and assurance.

Practicing Gratitude

Expressing gratitude, even in challenging circumstances, helps shift our focus from our problems to God's goodness and faithfulness. This practice can enhance our sense of peace and contentment.

Trusting in God's Sovereignty

Trusting in God's sovereignty and His control over our lives enables us to rest in His peace. Recognizing that God is in control and has a plan for us can reduce anxiety and fear.

Misunderstandings and Cautions

Misinterpreting the Source of Peace

It's important to remember that this peace is from God and not something we generate ourselves. Relying on our own efforts to achieve peace can lead to frustration and disappointment.

Overlooking the Role of Thanksgiving

While prayer is essential, thanksgiving is equally important. Focusing solely on presenting our requests without expressing gratitude can limit our experience of God's peace.

Ignoring the Need for a Relationship with Christ

God's peace is experienced "in Christ Jesus." A personal relationship with Jesus is foundational for accessing and maintaining this peace. Without this relationship, our efforts may fall short.

Biblical Examples

Jesus Calms the Storm

In Mark 4:35-41, Jesus calms a violent storm, demonstrating His authority over nature and His ability to bring peace in chaotic situations. The disciples' fear turns to awe as they witness Jesus' power, reminding us that Jesus is our source of peace in life's storms.

Paul and Silas in Prison

In Acts 16:16-40, Paul and Silas experience God's peace while imprisoned. Despite their dire circumstances, they pray and sing hymns to God. Their peaceful demeanor, even in suffering, leads to the conversion of the jailer and his household.

Hannah's Prayer

In 1 Samuel 1:1-20, Hannah pours out her heart to God in prayer, expressing her deep anguish over being childless. After praying and receiving assurance from Eli, the priest, she experiences peace and her countenance changes. God later answers her prayer with the birth of Samuel.

Conclusion

Philippians 4:7 offers a profound promise of God's peace that surpasses all understanding. As Christians, we are encouraged to bring our concerns to God in prayer and to practice gratitude, trusting in His sovereignty and goodness. By doing so, we can experience the peace of God that guards our hearts and minds in Christ Jesus. This divine peace not only provides comfort and assurance but also serves as a powerful testimony of God's presence and power in our lives.

Brand 316 Inc www.brand316.org 727 North Waco #290 Wichita KS 67203 (316) 247-2050

Reflective Questions – Answer in Writing

1. How do you currently experience the peace of God in your life, and in what areas do you struggle to find peace?

2. In what ways can you incorporate more prayer and thanksgiving into your daily routine to develop God's peace?

3. How does trusting in God's sovereignty help you to experience His peace, especially in difficult situations?

4. Reflect on a time when you experienced God's peace despite challenging circumstances. What did you learn from that experience?

5. How can you share the peace of God with others, and what practical steps can you take to be a source of peace and encouragement to those around you?

Week 31: Joseph: From a Pit to a Palace

The life of Joseph is a testament to the providence of God, His sovereignty over all circumstances, and His ability to transform adversity into triumph. From being sold into slavery by his own brothers to becoming a powerful ruler in Egypt, Joseph's journey is marked by resilience, forgiveness, and unwavering faith in God's plan. In this lesson, we will dive into the life of Joseph, examining his strengths, weaknesses, and the ways in which God used him for His glory.

Verse to Review: Genesis 50:20

"But as for you, you meant evil against me; but God meant it for good, in order to bring it about as it is this day, to save many people alive."

History of Joseph:

Joseph was the favored son of Jacob, born to him in his old age through Rachel, Jacob's beloved wife. His story begins with jealousy and betrayal as his brothers, consumed by envy, sold him into slavery. Despite facing numerous trials and injustices, Joseph remained faithful to God, eventually rising to prominence in Egypt and becoming a key figure in the fulfillment of God's plan to save His people from famine.

Joseph's Strengths and Flaws:

Joseph's greatest strength was his unwavering faith in God and his ability to maintain his integrity and character in the face of adversity. Despite being wronged by his brothers and unjustly imprisoned, Joseph remained faithful to God's plan and consistently demonstrated qualities of leadership, wisdom, and compassion. However, Joseph also had his flaws, including moments of pride and insensitivity towards others.

Joseph's Flaws Expanded:

1. **Pride:** Joseph displayed a sense of superiority and pride when he shared his dreams with his brothers, implying that he would rule over them one day (Genesis 37:5-11). This act of boasting contributed to his brothers' jealousy and ultimately led to their plot to sell him into slavery. Joseph's pride blinded him to the potential consequences of his actions and strained his relationships with his family.
2. **Vindictiveness:** When Joseph's brothers traveled to Egypt seeking food during the famine, Joseph recognized them but initially concealed his identity. He subjected them to a series of tests and accusations, including falsely accusing them of being spies and detaining his brother Simeon (Genesis 42:9-20). While Joseph eventually revealed himself to his brothers and forgave them, his initial actions reflect a vindictive streak, driven by his desire for retribution for the wrongs they had done to him in the past and likely a desire to not want to trust them or what they say.

125

3. **Naivety:** Joseph exhibited naivety in his interactions with Potiphar's wife. Despite her repeated advances, Joseph consistently refused her advances, demonstrating his commitment to moral integrity. However, his naivety was evident in his failure to recognize the extent of her deceitfulness. Instead of immediately removing himself from the situation or seeking help, Joseph remained in her presence, which ultimately led to false accusations of attempted rape and his unjust imprisonment (Genesis 39:6-20).

God's Redemption Through Joseph's Faith:

Despite his flaws and moments of weakness, God remained faithful to Joseph and used him as an instrument of His grace and redemption. Through Joseph's leadership and wisdom, God orchestrated the preservation of His people during a time of famine, ultimately leading to their reconciliation and restoration with Joseph and their father Jacob. Joseph's story serves as a powerful reminder of God's ability to bring beauty from ashes and to use even the darkest moments of our lives for His glory. We need to remind ourselves of this often – God is in control even when it feels empty or hopeless. Trust in Him.

Conclusion:

Joseph's story is a powerful reminder of the transformative power of forgiveness and reconciliation. Despite his flaws and moments of weakness, Joseph extended forgiveness to his brothers and sought reconciliation with them, ultimately leading to the restoration of their relationship and the preservation of their family. Joseph's journey challenges us to examine our own hearts and lives before God, acknowledging our own need for forgiveness and reconciliation with others.

One of the most significant lessons we can learn from Joseph's life is the importance of trusting in God's providence and sovereignty, even in the midst of adversity and uncertainty. Despite facing betrayal, injustice and hardship, Joseph remained faithful to God and His plan, knowing that God was able to bring about good from even the most difficult circumstances. Through Joseph's unwavering faith, God orchestrated the preservation of His people and the fulfillment of His promises, ultimately leading to their reconciliation and restoration.

Joseph's legacy of forgiveness and reconciliation endured beyond his lifetime, serving as a model for all who seek to follow God faithfully. Through his example, Joseph demonstrated the transformative power of forgiveness and reconciliation in healing broken relationships and restoring unity within families and communities.

In conclusion, Joseph's journey from pit to palace is a remarkable testament to the providence of God and His ability to transform adversity into triumph. As we reflect on Joseph's story, may we be challenged to trust in God's sovereignty and providence, knowing that He is able to redeem and restore even the most broken circumstances.

Reflective Questions - Answer in Writing

1. In what ways do Joseph's strengths and weaknesses resonate with your own experiences and struggles?

2. Reflect on a time when you struggled with pride or arrogance in your interactions with others. How did you overcome these challenges?

3. Consider Joseph's journey of forgiveness and reconciliation with his brothers. How can we cultivate a similar spirit of forgiveness and reconciliation in our own lives?

4. Despite his flaws and moments of weakness, Joseph remained faithful to God's plan. How does Joseph's story give you hope for your own journey of faith?

5. How can you trust in God's sovereignty and providence, like Joseph, in the midst of adversity and uncertainty?

2 Timothy 3:16 highlights the importance and authority of Scripture in the life of a believer. It is important to know and understand that all decisions in your life should be prayerfully and thoughtfully considered through the scripture. The Word of God equips us for every good work and guides our lives.

The Book of 2 Timothy

2 Timothy is an letter written by the Apostle Paul to his protégé Timothy. It is one of Paul's pastoral letters, offering guidance, encouragement, and instruction for church leadership and Christian living. **Written during Paul's imprisonment in Rome**, it is filled with urgency and profound personal reflections as he nears the end of his life.

Immediate Context

In 2 Timothy 3, Paul warns Timothy about the difficult times to come and the godlessness that will characterize the last days. He contrasts the behavior of false teachers with the life and teaching that Timothy has received. Paul emphasizes the importance of continuing in what he has learned and remaining rooted in the Scriptures.

Exploring 2 Timothy 3:16

The Text

"All Scripture is God-breathed and is useful for teaching, rebuking, correcting and training in righteousness." (2 Timothy 3:16, NIV)

Key Phrases

1. **"All Scripture"**

   o   This phrase signifies the entire Bible, both Old and New Testaments, affirming its comprehensive authority and relevance.

2. **"Is God-breathed"**

   o   This underscores the divine origin of Scripture, indicating that it is inspired by God. The term "God-breathed" (theopneustos in Greek) suggests that the Scriptures carry the breath, or Spirit, of God, making them uniquely authoritative and powerful.

3. **"Useful for teaching, rebuking, correcting and training in righteousness"**

   o   This phrase outlines the practical purposes of Scripture in the life of a believer:

- **Teaching**: Providing sound doctrine and instructing in truth.

- **Rebuking**: Confronting and exposing sin and error.

- **Correcting**: Guiding towards restoration and right living.

- **Training in righteousness**: Equipping and disciplining for a godly life.

Theological Implications

The Divine Inspiration of Scripture

The affirmation that all Scripture is "God-breathed" emphasizes its divine origin and authority. This means that the Bible is not merely a collection of human writings but is the very Word of God, carrying His authority and truth. This divine inspiration ensures that Scripture is flawless and trustworthy, providing a solid foundation for faith and practice.

The Comprehensive Usefulness of Scripture

Paul highlights four specific uses of Scripture, demonstrating its comprehensive role in the life of a believer. These functions underscore the practical relevance of the Bible for teaching sound doctrine, confronting sin, guiding towards correction, and training in righteousness. This comprehensive usefulness equips believers for every aspect of their spiritual journey and growth.

Practical Applications

Embracing the Authority of Scripture

- **Study Diligently**: Engage in regular and systematic study of the Bible. Seek to understand its teachings and allow them to shape your beliefs and actions.

- **Submit Humbly**: Recognize the authority of Scripture in all areas of life. Submit your thoughts, decisions, and behaviors to the teachings of the Bible, allowing it to guide and correct you.

Utilizing Scripture for Growth

- **Teaching**: Use Scripture to learn and teach others sound doctrine. Engage in Bible studies, discussions, and teachings that are rooted in the Word of God.

- **Rebuking**: Allow Scripture to confront and expose areas of sin and error in your life. Be open to correction and seek to align your life with God's standards.

- **Correcting**: Use the guidance of Scripture to restore and redirect your life towards righteousness. Seek biblical counsel and apply its principles to your daily decisions.

- **Training in Righteousness**: Let Scripture be your guide for living a godly life. Apply its teachings to your personal growth, relationships, and daily conduct.

Misunderstandings and Cautions

Misinterpreting Scripture

Avoid taking verses out of context or interpreting Scripture to fit personal agendas. Seek to understand the historical and literary context of passages and interpret them with the overall message of the Bible.

Neglecting Parts of Scripture

Do not neglect parts of the Bible that are challenging or uncomfortable. All Scripture is valuable and necessary for a complete understanding of God's will and character.

Biblical Examples

Jesus' Use of Scripture

Jesus demonstrated the authority and usefulness of Scripture in His ministry. In Matthew 4:1-11, during His temptation in the wilderness, Jesus used Scripture to counter the devil's temptations, emphasizing its power and authority.

The Bereans

In Acts 17:10-12, the Berean Jews are commended for their noble character as they received Paul's message with eagerness and examined the Scriptures daily to see if what Paul said was true. Their diligent study and application of Scripture serve as a model for believers.

Timothy's Upbringing

In 2 Timothy 1:5 and 3:14-15, Paul refers to Timothy's upbringing in the Scriptures, taught by his mother and grandmother. This foundation equipped Timothy for his ministry and highlights the importance of being rooted in the Word from a young age.

Conclusion

2 Timothy 3:16 offers a profound affirmation of the divine inspiration and comprehensive usefulness of Scripture. Christians are called to embrace the authority of Scripture and utilize it for teaching, rebuking, correcting, and training in righteousness. Let us commit to a life rooted in the Word of God, allowing it to shape our beliefs, guide our actions, and transform our lives.

Reflective Questions – Answer in Writing

1. How does understanding the divine inspiration of Scripture impact your view of the Bible?

2. How can you deepen your study and application of Scripture in your life? (list them out)

3. How can you use Scripture to teach, rebuke, correct, and train in righteousness within your community?

4. What challenges do you face in submitting to the authority of Scripture, and how can you overcome them?

5. How does the comprehensive usefulness of Scripture equip you for every good work and guide your spiritual growth?

131

James 3:9 addresses the profound inconsistency in human speech, highlighting the double nature of our words. This verse emphasizes the importance of using our tongues to bless rather than curse. It is important for Christians to recognize the power of our words and strive for consistency in our speech as followers of Christ.

The Book of James

The Book of James is a practical guide for Christian living, written by James, the brother of Jesus. It covers various topics, including faith and works, taming the tongue, and living wisely. James is known for its direct and clear instructions on how to live a life that reflects genuine faith.

Immediate Context

James 3 focuses on the power of the tongue and the challenge of controlling it. Verses 1-12 discuss the impact of our words and the difficulty of taming the tongue. James uses vivid imagery to illustrate how small the tongue is, yet how powerful it can be in influencing our lives and the lives of others.

Exploring James 3:9

The Text

"With the tongue we praise our Lord and Father, and with it we curse human beings, who have been made in God's likeness" (James 3:9, NIV).

Key Phrases

1. **"With the tongue we praise our Lord and Father"**

   o   This phrase highlights the positive use of the tongue. Praising God is one of the highest forms of speech, acknowledging His greatness and expressing our worship and gratitude. In all things we do, we should be praising God!

2. **"With it we curse human beings"**

   o   This phrase contrasts the previous one, showing the negative use of the tongue. Cursing others involves speaking harmful, disrespectful, or hateful words against them.

3. **"Who have been made in God's likeness"**

   o   This phrase emphasizes the inherent value and dignity of every human being. As beings made in the image of God, we deserve to be treated with respect and honor.

Brand 316 Inc www.brand316.org 727 North Waco #290 Wichita KS 67203 (316) 247-2050

Theological Implications

The Power of the Tongue

James 3:9 underscores the power of the tongue to both bless and curse. Our words can uplift and praise God, but they can also harm and demean others. Recognizing this dual capability encourages us to use our speech responsibly. It is important to remind ourselves how powerful words can be.

The Inconsistency of Human Speech

The verse highlights the inconsistency in human speech—praising God while cursing those made in His image. This inconsistency reflects a deeper issue in our hearts and calls us to strive for alignment between our words and our faith.

The Value of Human Beings

James reminds us that every person is made in God's likeness, emphasizing the importance of treating others with respect and dignity. Our words should reflect this truth, honoring the inherent worth of every person.

Practical Applications

Speaking with Consistency

Aim for consistency in your speech. Let your words reflect your faith in all situations, whether you are praising God or interacting with others. Strive to eliminate harmful speech and cultivate a habit of speaking blessings.

Respecting Others

Recognize the value of every person you interact with. Treat others with the same respect and honor that you would show to God. Avoid words that demean, belittle, or harm others, remembering that they are made in God's image.

Guarding Your Heart

Since our words reflect the condition of our hearts, focus on cultivating a heart that aligns with God's values. Spend time in prayer, scripture, and self-reflection to address any attitudes or beliefs that lead to harmful speech.

Misunderstandings and Cautions

Ignoring the Impact of Words

It can be easy to overlook the impact of our words, especially in casual or heated conversations. Be mindful that even seemingly insignificant words can have a profound effect on others.

Justifying Harmful Speech

Sometimes, we might justify harmful speech by claiming it is deserved or by downplaying its significance. All people are made in God's likeness and deserve to be spoken to with respect and love.

Overlooking Personal Responsibility

While it is important to encourage others to speak kindly, we must also take personal responsibility for our own words. Regularly evaluate your speech and seek to align it with God's standards.

Biblical Examples

Peter's Denial

In Matthew 26:69-75, Peter denies knowing Jesus three times. His words reflected fear and self-preservation rather than faithfulness to Jesus. This incident shows how our speech can betray our true feelings and impact our witness.

Jesus and the Woman Caught in Adultery

In John 8:1-11, Jesus uses His words to protect and restore the woman caught in adultery. Instead of condemning her, He offers grace and a call to repentance. Jesus' example demonstrates the power of words to heal and uplift.

David and Nathan

In 2 Samuel 12:1-14, the prophet Nathan confronts King David about his sin with Bathsheba. Nathan's words are direct and convicting, leading David to repentance. This story highlights the importance of using words to speak truth and bring about positive change.

Conclusion

James 3:9 challenges us to reflect on the consistency of our speech and its impact on others. We have the power to align our words with our faith, using them to bless rather than curse. As Christians, we are called to recognize the power of the tongue, respect the value of every human being, and strive for consistency in our speech. Let us focus on speaking words that reflect our faith, honor others, and build up the community of believers. By doing so, we can demonstrate the power of Christ in our lives.

Reflective Questions – Answer in Writing

1. How can you ensure that your speech consistently reflects your faith in both praising God and interacting with others?

2. What steps can you take to cultivate a heart that aligns with God's values, resulting in positive and respectful speech?

3. Reflect on a time when your words either uplifted or harmed someone. What did you learn from that experience, and how can it guide your future interactions?

4. How can you actively respect and honor the value of every person you interact with through your words?

5. In what ways can you encourage and model positive speech within your faith community, promoting a culture of blessing and respect?

Week 34: The Apostle Paul: A Life Transformed by Grace

The Apostle Paul, formerly known as Saul of Tarsus, is one of the most influential figures in Christian history. His life exemplifies the transformative power of God's grace and the profound impact of encountering Jesus Christ. In this lesson, we will explore the life of the Apostle Paul, examining his strengths, weaknesses, and the journey that led him from persecutor to preacher of the gospel.

Verse to Review: Acts 9:3-6

"As he neared Damascus on his journey, suddenly a light from heaven flashed around him. He fell to the ground and heard a voice say to him, 'Saul, Saul, why do you persecute me?' 'Who are you, Lord?' Saul asked. 'I am Jesus, whom you are persecuting,' he replied."

Background of the Apostle Paul:

The Apostle Paul was born as Saul of Tarsus, a devout Pharisee and zealous persecutor of the early Christian church. He played a significant role in the persecution of Christians, overseeing their arrest, imprisonment and murder. However, his life was dramatically transformed when he encountered Jesus Christ on the road to Damascus, leading to his conversion and commissioning as an apostle to the Gentiles.

Strengths and Flaws of the Apostle Paul:

Some of his strengths include:

1. **Zeal and Passion:** Paul exhibited great zeal and passion in his pursuit of truth and righteousness, initially directed towards the persecution of Christians. However, after his conversion, his zeal was redirected towards preaching the gospel and advancing the kingdom of God.
2. **Intellectual Depth and Scriptural Knowledge:** One of Paul's greatest strengths was his profound intellectual depth and extensive knowledge of the Scriptures. As a highly educated Pharisee and scholar of Jewish law, Paul possessed a deep understanding of the Old Testament scriptures, which he adeptly utilized in his teachings and writings. His letters to various early Christian communities are marked by theological depth, doctrinal clarity, and profound insights into the nature of God's redemptive plan. Paul's ability to engage with complex theological concepts and articulate them in a clear and accessible manner played a crucial role in shaping the doctrinal foundation of the early Christian church.
3. **Courage and Perseverance:** Another notable strength of Paul was his unwavering passion and zealous commitment to spreading the gospel message. From his dramatic conversion on the road to Damascus to his tireless missionary journeys across the Mediterranean world, Paul demonstrated an unparalleled zeal for proclaiming the good news of Jesus Christ to both Jews and Gentiles alike. Despite facing numerous hardships, including persecution, imprisonment,

Brand 316 Inc www.brand316.org 727 North Waco #290 Wichita KS 67203 (316) 247-2050

and opposition from both religious authorities and hostile crowds, Paul remained steadfast in his resolve to fulfill his calling as an apostle and evangelist. His relentless perseverance in the face of adversity serves as a compelling example of dedication and devotion to the cause of Christ.

4. **Spiritual Insight and Discernment:** Paul possessed a remarkable gift of spiritual insight and discernment, evidenced by his ability to discern the workings of the Holy Spirit and discern the spiritual condition of individuals and communities. Throughout his ministry, Paul demonstrated a keen awareness of the spiritual battles being waged and the need for believers to stand firm in the face of temptation and spiritual deception. His letters often contain exhortations to spiritual maturity, warnings against false teachings, and instructions for righteous living. Paul's discerning wisdom and spiritual insight continue to serve as invaluable guides for Christians navigating the complexities of the Christian life and spiritual warfare.

5. **Adaptability and Flexibility:** Another strength of Paul was his adaptability and flexibility in ministry. Throughout his missionary journeys, Paul encountered a wide range of cultural contexts, religious beliefs, and social dynamics. Rather than rigidly adhering to a fixed methodology, Paul demonstrated a willingness to adapt his approach and strategies to effectively engage with different audiences and address their unique needs and concerns. Whether circumcising Timothy to facilitate ministry among Jews or participating in the religious practices of the Athenians to connect with them, Paul's adaptability enabled him to effectively bridge cultural divides and establish meaningful relationships with diverse communities.

Some of his weaknesses include:

1. **Persecution of Christians:** Before his conversion, Paul was complicit in the persecution and imprisonment of early Christians, consenting to the stoning of Stephen and actively seeking to destroy the fledgling Christian movement. His misguided zeal and religious fervor blinded him to the truth of Jesus Christ.

2. **Impatience and Frustration:** At times, Paul's passion and zeal for the gospel could manifest as impatience and frustration, especially when dealing with the spiritual immaturity or resistance of fellow believers. In his letters, Paul occasionally expresses exasperation with the behavior of some individuals or communities, urging them to mature in their faith and understanding. For example, in his letter to the Corinthians, Paul chastises them for their divisions and immorality, displaying a sense of frustration with their lack of spiritual progress (1 Corinthians 3:1-3).

3. **Physical Weakness and Afflictions:** Paul's ministry was marked by numerous physical hardships and afflictions, including beatings, imprisonment, shipwrecks, and chronic health issues. In his second letter to the Corinthians, Paul speaks candidly about his "thorn in the flesh," a mysterious affliction that tormented him and which he pleaded with God to remove (2 Corinthians 12:7-10). While Paul's weaknesses and sufferings served to highlight God's strength and grace, they also posed significant challenges and limitations in his ministry and personal life.

Brand 316 Inc www.brand316.org 727 North Waco #290 Wichita KS 67203 (316) 247-2050

4. **Struggle with Loneliness and Isolation:** Despite his extensive travels and ministry engagements, Paul often experienced periods of loneliness and isolation in his ministry. His frequent relocations and separations from close companions, coupled with the demands of his apostolic responsibilities, could leave him feeling isolated and emotionally drained. In his letters, Paul occasionally expresses feelings of loneliness and longing for companionship, urging his fellow believers to visit him or send companions to minister to him (2 Timothy 4:9-13). Paul's experiences of loneliness highlight the human aspect of his ministry and serve as a reminder of the importance of community and fellowship in the Christian life.

God's Response to the Apostle Paul:

Despite Paul's past as a persecutor of the church and his struggles with pride and contention, God responded to him with grace and mercy. He does the same for you and I. Through a supernatural encounter on the road to Damascus, Jesus Christ revealed Himself to Paul, transforming his life and commissioning him as an apostle to the Gentiles. Paul's conversion experience serves as a powerful testimony to the transformative power of encountering the risen Christ. It is important to remember that you serve a God of second chances; Paul is a great example of this.

The story of the Apostle Paul offers valuable lessons for believers today, reminding us of the boundless grace and mercy of God and the transformative power of encountering Jesus Christ. His strengths and weaknesses serve as a reminder that God's grace is sufficient to overcome our shortcomings and empower us for His service.

Conclusion:

The Apostle Paul's life is a remarkable testimony to the transformative power of God's grace and the boundless potential for redemption in Christ. His journey from persecutor to preacher of the gospel serves as a powerful reminder that no one is beyond the reach of God's love and mercy, and that even the most unlikely candidates can be used by God for His purposes.

Moreover, the Apostle Paul's ministry provides a model of effective evangelism and discipleship for believers today. His zeal for the gospel, combined with his intellectual depth and theological insight, enabled him to effectively communicate the message of salvation to diverse audiences and cultures. His letters, inspired by the Holy Spirit, continue to instruct, encourage, and challenge believers in their faith and witness. Paul's background made his testimony stronger and was used to glorify God.

Furthermore, the Apostle Paul's life exemplifies the importance of perseverance and endurance in the Christian journey. Despite facing numerous hardships and opposition, including persecution, imprisonment, and shipwrecks, Paul remained steadfast in his commitment to proclaiming the gospel and advancing the kingdom of God. His example inspires believers to persevere in the face of adversity, trusting in God's strength and faithfulness to sustain them through every trial.

In conclusion, the Apostle Paul's life is a testament to the transformative power of encountering Jesus Christ and the boundless grace and mercy of God. His strengths and weaknesses serve as a reminder that God's grace is sufficient to overcome our shortcomings and empower us for His service.

Reflective Questions - Answer in Writing

1. In what ways do you see yourself in the strengths and weaknesses of the Apostle Paul?

2. Reflect on a time when you experienced a transformative encounter with Jesus Christ. How did this impact your life and ministry?

3. Consider the Apostle Paul's struggles with pride and contention. How can you guard against similar pitfalls in your own life and ministry?

4. Reflect on God's response to the Apostle Paul's past as a persecutor of the church. How does this demonstrate His boundless grace and mercy?

5. How does the story of the Apostle Paul challenge you to live a life of faith and obedience, trusting in God's grace and empowering for His service?

Mark 9:42 is a powerful verse that emphasizes the seriousness of leading others, especially the vulnerable, into sin. Jesus uses strong language to convey the importance of being mindful of our actions and their impact on others. Mark 9:42 helps guide us to understand the weight of our influence and the responsibility we have towards others.

The Gospel of Mark

The Gospel of Mark is one of the four Gospels in the New Testament, providing a vivid account of Jesus' life, teachings, miracles, death, and resurrection. Mark's Gospel is known for its fast-paced narrative and emphasis on the actions of Jesus.

Immediate Context

In Mark 9:33-50, Jesus is teaching His disciples about humility, the seriousness of sin, and the importance of leading by example. The disciples had been arguing about who among them was the greatest. Jesus responds by teaching them about servanthood and the severe consequences of causing others to stumble in their faith.

Exploring Mark 9:42

The Text

"If anyone causes one of these little ones—those who believe in me—to stumble, it would be better for them if a large millstone were hung around their neck and they were thrown into the sea" (Mark 9:42, NIV).

Key Phrases

1. **"If anyone causes one of these little ones"**

   o "Little ones" refers to those who are vulnerable in their faith, including children and new believers. Jesus highlights the importance of protecting and nurturing their spiritual growth.

2. **"To stumble"**

   o To cause someone to stumble means to lead them into sin or to hinder their faith. Jesus is warning against actions that could cause others to fall away from their relationship with Him.

3. **"It would be better for them if a large millstone were hung around their neck and they were thrown into the sea"**

   o This hyperbolic statement underscores the severity of leading others into sin. A millstone was a heavy stone used for grinding grain, and being thrown into the sea with such a weight would ensure drowning. Jesus uses this drastic imagery to emphasize the gravity of the offense.

Theological Implications

The Responsibility of Influence

Mark 9:42 highlights the responsibility we have in influencing others. Our actions, words, and attitudes can either build up or tear down the faith of others. This verse calls us to be mindful of our impact on those who look to us for guidance.

The Value of the Vulnerable

Jesus places great value on "little ones"—those who are vulnerable in their faith. Protecting and nurturing their spiritual growth is paramount. This reflects God's heart for the weak and His desire for the spiritual well-being of all believers.

The Seriousness of Sin

The severe imagery used by Jesus underscores the seriousness of leading others into sin. It serves as a stark reminder that sin is not to be taken lightly, and we must be vigilant in our conduct to avoid causing others to stumble.

Practical Applications

Mindful of Our Actions

Evaluate your actions and words, considering how they might impact others, especially those who are vulnerable in their faith. Strive to live in a way that builds up and encourages others in their walk with Christ.

Protecting the Vulnerable

Take active steps to protect and nurture the faith of new believers and children. Provide support, encouragement, and sound teaching to help them grow in their relationship with God.

Leading by Example

Lead by example in your faith community. Demonstrate humility, integrity, and love in your actions, setting a example for others to follow. Be a source of encouragement and strength to those around you.

Misunderstandings and Cautions

Misinterpreting the Severity

The hyperbolic nature of Jesus' statement is meant to underscore the seriousness of causing others to stumble, not to suggest a literal punishment. Understand this imagery as a way to highlight the gravity of the offense, not as a prescription for action.

Neglecting Personal Responsibility

While it's important to be mindful of our influence on others, each person also has personal responsibility for their own faith journey. Encourage others to take ownership of their relationship with God, while still offering support and guidance.

Balancing Grace and Accountability

Maintain a balance between extending grace and holding others accountable. While it's important to address harmful behavior, do so with a spirit of love and restoration, reflecting the grace and forgiveness of Christ. It is important to remember we serve a God of second chances.

Biblical Examples

Peter's Denial

In Luke 22:54-62, Peter denies knowing Jesus three times, causing potential stumbling for those who looked up to him as a disciple. However, Peter's later repentance and restoration illustrate the importance of owning one's mistakes and seeking forgiveness.

The Pharisees' Hypocrisy

In Matthew 23, Jesus rebukes the Pharisees for their hypocrisy, which led others astray. Their outward appearance of righteousness masked their sinful behavior, causing others to stumble. This highlights the danger of leading others into sin through hypocrisy.

The Influence of Timothy

In 1 Timothy 4:12, Paul encourages Timothy to set an example for believers in speech, conduct, love, faith, and purity. Timothy's positive influence on others demonstrates the impact of leading by example and nurturing the faith of others.

Conclusion

Mark 9:42 offers a sobering reminder of the responsibility believers have in influencing others, especially those who are vulnerable in their faith. By understanding its context, meaning, and practical applications, we can be vigilant in our conduct and protect the spiritual well-being of those around us.

As Christians, we are called to be mindful of our actions, protect the vulnerable, and lead by example. By doing so, we reflect Christ's love and nurture the faith of others. Let us commit to living in a way that builds up and encourages those who look to us for guidance, avoiding actions that could cause others to stumble.

Reflective Questions – Answer in Writing

1. How can you be more mindful of your actions and their impact on others, especially those who are vulnerable in their faith?

2. What steps can you take to protect and nurture the faith of new believers?

3. Reflect on a time when someone else's actions influenced your faith journey. How did it impact you, and what can you learn from that experience?

4. How can you lead by example in your faith community, demonstrating humility, integrity, and love?

5. How can you balance grace and holding others accountable in a way that reflects Christ's love and forgiveness?

Colossians 3:16 emphasizes the importance of letting Christ's message dwell among believers richly, encouraging teaching, and mutual admonition with wisdom. This verse highlights the role of Scripture in guiding Christian living and the significance of worship in building a strong faith community.

The Book of Colossians

The Book of Colossians is one of Paul's epistles, written to the church in Colossae. Paul wrote this letter to address false teachings and to encourage the believers to live out their new identity in Christ. The letter emphasizes the supremacy of Christ and the fullness of life found in Him.

Immediate Context

Colossians 3 focuses on the new life in Christ, urging believers to set their hearts on things above and to put to death earthly desires. Verses 12-17 outline the characteristics of a Christian community, emphasizing virtues like compassion, kindness, humility, and love. Verse 16, nestled in this passage, stresses the importance of Scripture and worship in fostering these virtues.

Exploring Colossians 3:16

The Text

"Let the message of Christ dwell among you richly as you teach and admonish one another with all wisdom through psalms, hymns, and songs from the Spirit, singing to God with gratitude in your hearts." (Colossians 3:16, NIV)

Key Phrases

1. **"Let the message of Christ dwell among you richly"**

   o This phrase encourages believers to immerse themselves in the teachings of Christ, allowing His message to saturate every aspect of their lives and community.

2. **"Teach and admonish one another with all wisdom"**

   o Paul highlights the importance of mutual instruction and correction within the Christian community, done with wisdom and care.

3. **"Through psalms, hymns, and songs from the Spirit"**

   o Worship through music is emphasized as a means of teaching and encouraging one another, allowing the Spirit to inspire and guide the community's worship.

4. **"Singing to God with gratitude in your hearts"**

   o   The attitude of gratitude is central to worship, reflecting a heart that is thankful for God's grace and blessings.

Theological Implications

The Centrality of Christ's Message

Christ's message, captured in the gospel, is the foundation of Christian teaching and living. Allowing this message to dwell richly among believers ensures that their lives and community are rooted in the truth of the gospel.

The Role of Mutual Teaching and Admonition

Teaching and admonishing one another are essential practices in a healthy Christian community. These activities, grounded in wisdom, help believers grow in their faith and maintain a Christ-centered life.

The Significance of Worship

Worship, particularly through music, plays a vital role in the life of the church. It serves as a vehicle for teaching, encouragement, and expressing gratitude to God. Worship brings the community together and aligns their hearts with God's purposes.

The Attitude of Gratitude

Gratitude is a defining characteristic of Christian worship and living. It reflects an awareness of God's grace and fosters a positive, joyful outlook among believers.

Practical Applications

Immersing in Christ's Message

- **Daily Scripture Reading**: Commit to reading and meditating on the Bible daily, allowing Christ's message to dwell richly in your heart.

- **Bible Study Groups**: Join or lead a Bible study group to explore and discuss Scripture with others, deepening your understanding and application of God's Word. You can use these lessons as a group Bible study.

Teaching and Admonishing with Wisdom

- **Encouragement and Correction**: Encourage and **_gently_** correct fellow believers, using wisdom and love to guide your interactions.

- **Seek Wisdom**: Pray for wisdom in your teaching and admonition, ensuring your words are edifying and aligned with God's truth.

Engaging in Worship

- **Participate in Musical Worship**: Engage actively in musical worship during church services, allowing the songs to teach and inspire you.

- **Personal Worship Time**: Incorporate worship through music in your personal devotional time, singing psalms, hymns, and spiritual songs to God.

Cultivating Gratitude

- **Gratitude Journals**: Keep a gratitude journal to regularly record and reflect on God's blessings, fostering a thankful heart.

- **Express Gratitude**: Regularly express your gratitude to God in prayer and worship, acknowledging His goodness and grace in your life.

Misunderstandings and Cautions

Overlooking the Richness of Christ's Message

Avoid reducing Christ's message to a set of rules or doctrines. Embrace the fullness and depth of the gospel, allowing it to transform every aspect of your life.

Misusing Admonition

Admonition should be done with wisdom and love, not harshness or judgment. Ensure that your corrections are aimed at building up and restoring, not tearing down.

Neglecting the Heart in Worship

Worship is not just about outward expressions but the attitude of the heart. Ensure that your worship is genuine and stems from a heart of gratitude and love for God.

Biblical Examples

Early Christian Community

In Acts 2:42-47, the early Christian community devoted themselves to the apostles' teaching, fellowship, breaking of bread, and prayer. They shared everything, met each other's needs, and worshiped together, embodying the principles outlined in Colossians 3:16.

Paul and Silas in Prison

Brand 316 Inc www.brand316.org 727 North Waco #290 Wichita KS 67203 (316) 247-2050

In Acts 16:25, Paul and Silas, imprisoned in Philippi, sang hymns to God despite their circumstances. Their worship not only sustained them but also impacted the other prisoners and led to the jailer's conversion, demonstrating the power of worship and gratitude.

King David

King David, known for his psalms, exemplified a heart of worship and gratitude. His life, filled with ups and downs, consistently reflected a deep reliance on God and a commitment to worship through music and prayer, as seen throughout the Psalms.

Conclusion

Colossians 3:16 provides profound guidance for living out the Christian faith within a community. We are called to immerse ourselves in Christ's message, teach and admonish one another with wisdom, engage in heartfelt worship and cultivate gratitude. Commit to living out these principles, allowing Christ's message to dwell richly among us and transform our lives. By doing so, we reflect the beauty and power of the gospel in our communities and the world.

Reflective Questions – Answer in Writing

1. How can you ensure that Christ's message dwells richly in your daily life?

2. What practical steps can you take to teach and admonish others with wisdom and love?

3. How can you incorporate worship into your personal and communal spiritual practices?

4. In what ways can you develop a heart of gratitude in your daily life?

5. How can you encourage and support others in your community to live out the principles of Colossians 3:16?

Week 37: Jonah: A Story of Redemption and Mercy

The story of Jonah is a timeless tale of God's mercy and the transformative power of obedience. Despite his initial reluctance and disobedience, Jonah ultimately became a vessel for God's message of repentance and salvation to the people of Nineveh. In this lesson, we will explore the life of Jonah, examining his strengths, weaknesses, and the ways in which God used him for His glory.

Verse to Review: Jonah 1:3

"But Jonah ran away from the Lord and headed for Tarshish."

History of Jonah:

Jonah was a prophet of the Northern Kingdom of Israel during the reign of King Jeroboam II. He is best known for his mission to the city of Nineveh, the capital of the Assyrian Empire. Despite being called by God to preach a message of repentance to the people of Nineveh, Jonah initially attempted to flee from God's presence by boarding a ship bound for Tarshish. However, God intervened, sending a great storm that ultimately led to Jonah's repentance and obedience to God's command. Jonah's story is much more than being swallowed by a great fish.

Jonah's Strengths and Flaws:

Jonah's greatest strength was his deep faith and reverence for God. As a prophet, Jonah was entrusted with delivering God's messages to His people, and he remained faithful to this calling throughout his life. However, Jonah also had his flaws, particularly his stubbornness and lack of compassion. His initial refusal to obey God's command to preach to the people of Nineveh stemmed from his prejudice and resentment towards them, as well as his fear of their potential repentance and God's forgiveness.

Jonah's initial response to God's call to preach to the people of Nineveh was one of stubbornness and disobedience. Instead of obeying God's command, Jonah attempted to flee from His presence by boarding a ship bound for Tarshish. Jonah's disobedience not only endangered his own life but also jeopardized the lives of those around him, as evidenced by the great storm that God sent to thwart his escape (Jonah 1:3-4).

Jonah's reluctance to preach to the people of Nineveh was rooted in his prejudice and lack of compassion towards them. As an Israelite, Jonah harbored deep-seated animosity towards the Assyrians, who were known for their cruelty and oppression. Jonah's unwillingness to extend God's message of repentance and salvation to the people of Nineveh reflected his narrow-mindedness and lack of understanding of God's mercy and grace.

Jonah's reaction to God's mercy towards the people of Nineveh revealed his own resentment and bitterness towards God's character. Instead of rejoicing over the repentance of the Ninevites and God's

148

forgiveness towards them, Jonah became angry and resentful, questioning God's justice and righteousness (Jonah 4:1-3). Jonah's response highlights his failure to fully grasp the depth of God's love and mercy towards all people, regardless of their nationality or background.

God's Redemption Through Jonah's Obedience:

Despite Jonah's flaws and shortcomings, God remained faithful to His plan and used Jonah to bring about repentance and salvation to the people of Nineveh. Through a series of miraculous events, including Jonah's deliverance from the belly of a great fish and his subsequent preaching to the Ninevites, God demonstrated His sovereignty and mercy. The people of Nineveh responded to Jonah's message with genuine repentance and God relented from bringing judgment upon them.

Conclusion:

Jonah's journey from reluctant prophet to obedient servant is a powerful testament to God's mercy and grace. Despite his flaws and shortcomings, God remained faithful to His plan and used Jonah to accomplish His purposes. Through a series of miraculous events, including Jonah's deliverance from the belly of a great fish and his subsequent preaching to the people of Nineveh, God demonstrated His sovereignty and power over all creation.

One of the most significant lessons we can learn from Jonah's story is the importance of obedience and humility in responding to God's call. Despite his initial reluctance and disobedience, Jonah ultimately obeyed God's command and preached a message of repentance to the people of Nineveh. His obedience not only led to the salvation of countless lives but also served as a testimony to God's mercy and compassion towards all people.

Jonah's response to God's mercy towards the people of Nineveh also serves as a sobering reminder of the danger of harboring resentment and prejudice in our own hearts. Instead of rejoicing over the repentance of the Ninevites and God's forgiveness towards them, Jonah became angry and resentful, questioning God's justice and righteousness. Jonah's response highlights the danger of allowing bitterness and prejudice to cloud our judgment and hinder our ability to extend God's love and mercy to others. We serve a God of second chances. Let's embrace God's call to extend His love and mercy to all people, knowing that He desires for none to perish but for all to come to repentance.

Jonah's story is a powerful reminder of God's mercy and the transformative power of obedience. That is something we all need. Despite his initial reluctance and disobedience, Jonah ultimately became a vessel for God's message of repentance and salvation to the people of Nineveh. As we reflect on Jonah's story, may we be challenged to examine our own hearts and attitudes towards those who may seem different from us. May we, like Jonah, embrace God's call to extend His love and mercy to all people, knowing that He desires for none to perish but for all to come to repentance.

Brand 316 Inc www.brand316.org 727 North Waco #290 Wichita KS 67203 (316) 247-2050

Reflective Questions - Answer in Writing

1. In what ways do Jonah's flaws and shortcomings resonate with your own struggles and challenges?

2. Reflect on a time when you were called to step out in obedience, despite your own reluctance or fear. How did God use that experience to shape and transform you?

3. Consider Jonah's response to God's mercy towards the people of Nineveh. How can we cultivate a spirit of compassion and humility in our own lives?

4. Despite his initial disobedience, God still used Jonah to bring about repentance and salvation to the people of Nineveh. How does this give you hope for your own journey of faith?

5. How can you align your heart and attitudes more closely with God's desire for all people to experience His mercy and salvation?

Week 38: Ephesians 4:31-32 - Forgiveness and Kindness in Christ

Ephesians 4:31-32 is a passage that teaches about the importance of letting go of negative behaviors and embracing a Christ-like attitude of kindness, compassion, and forgiveness. We will explore it to help us understand how to have healthy relationships and reflect God's love in our interactions with others.

The Book of Ephesians

The Book of Ephesians is a letter written by the Apostle Paul to the church in Ephesus. It addresses the spiritual blessings believers have in Christ and provides practical instructions for living a life worthy of the gospel. The letter emphasizes the unity of the church, the new life in Christ and the importance of ethical conduct.

Immediate Context

Ephesians 4 focuses on Christian conduct and unity. Paul encourages believers to live in a manner worthy of their calling, emphasizing qualities like humility, gentleness, patience, and love. Verses 25-32 specifically address behaviors that should be put away and attitudes that should be embraced in order to foster healthy, loving relationships within the body of Christ.

Exploring Ephesians 4:31-32

The Text

"Get rid of all bitterness, rage and anger, brawling and slander, along with every form of malice. Be kind and compassionate to one another, forgiving each other, just as in Christ God forgave you" (Ephesians 4:31-32, NIV).

Key Phrases

1. **"Get rid of all bitterness, rage and anger, brawling and slander, along with every form of malice"**

   o This phrase lists negative behaviors that believers are to stay away from. These attitudes and actions are destructive to relationships and hurt spiritual growth.

2. **"Be kind and compassionate to one another"**

   o Paul instructs believers to cultivate kindness and compassion. These positive attitudes reflect Christ's love and raise unity and harmony within the community.

3. **"Forgiving each other, just as in Christ God forgave you"**

- Forgiveness is essential in Christian relationships. Paul reminds believers that their forgiveness of others should mirror the forgiveness they have received from God through Christ.

Theological Implications

Transformation in Christ

Ephesians 4:31-32 highlights the power of the gospel. Believers are called to put off their old, sinful behaviors and embrace a new way of living that reflects Christ's character.

The Importance of Relationships

The passage emphasizes the importance of healthy, loving relationships within the body of Christ. Negative behaviors like bitterness and anger destroy relationships, while kindness, compassion, and forgiveness build and strengthen them.

Forgiveness as a Central Theme

Forgiveness is a central theme in the Christian faith. Just as believers have been forgiven by God through Christ, we are called to extend forgiveness to others, creating resolution and unity.

Practical Applications

Identifying and Eliminating Negative Behaviors

Christians should regularly examine their attitudes and actions, identifying any bitterness, anger, or malice that may be present. By seeking God's help and committing to change, they can put away these negative behaviors and cultivate a Christ-like character.

Cultivating Kindness and Compassion

Practicing kindness and compassion involves actively looking for opportunities to serve and care for others. Simple acts of kindness and a compassionate attitude can significantly impact relationships and reflect God's love.

Practicing Forgiveness

Forgiveness is not always easy, but it is essential for healthy relationships. Believers should remember the forgiveness they have received from God and extend that same grace to others, even when it is difficult.

Misunderstandings and Cautions

Misinterpreting Forgiveness

Forgiveness does not mean ignoring wrongdoing or allowing harmful behavior to continue. It involves letting go of resentment and choosing to release the offender, while also seeking justice and accountability where necessary.

Overlooking the Need for Personal Change

It's important to recognize that the call to eliminate negative behaviors applies to all believers. We must each take responsibility for our attitudes and actions, rather than focusing on the behavior of others.

Balancing Kindness with Truth

While kindness and compassion are essential, they should be balanced with truth. Loving others sometimes involves speaking the truth in love, addressing harmful behaviors, and encouraging growth and change.

Biblical Examples

Joseph and His Brothers

The story of Joseph and his brothers (Genesis 37-50) illustrates the power of forgiveness and reconciliation. Despite being sold into slavery by his brothers, Joseph forgives them and provides for their needs during a famine. His kindness and compassion reflect the principles in Ephesians 4:31-32.

David and Saul

David's relationship with King Saul (1 Samuel 18-26) exemplifies the importance of rejecting bitterness and malice. Despite Saul's attempts to kill him, David consistently shows kindness and refuses to harm Saul, demonstrating a Christ-like attitude.

The Prodigal Son

The parable of the Prodigal Son (Luke 15:11-32) highlights the themes of forgiveness and compassion. The father's joyful acceptance of his repentant son mirrors God's forgiveness of believers and serves as a model for how we should forgive others.

Conclusion

Ephesians 4:31-32 calls believers to put away negative behaviors and embrace kindness, compassion, and forgiveness.

As Christians, we are called to reject bitterness, anger, and malice, choosing instead to be kind, compassionate, and forgiving. Let us aim to live out these principles in our daily lives, creating unity and love within the body of Christ. By doing so, we reflect the transformative power of the gospel and honor the forgiveness we have received from God through Christ.

Brand 316 Inc www.brand316.org 727 North Waco #290 Wichita KS 67203 (316) 247-2050

Reflective Questions - Answer in Writing

1. Are there people you need to forgive? Are there people you need to ask for forgiveness?

2. Reflect on the negative emotions and behaviors mentioned in the passage. In what ways do these attitudes hinder Christian unity and fellowship?

3. Consider the virtues of kindness, compassion, and forgiveness highlighted in Ephesians 4:31-32. How can you grow these virtues in your interactions with others?

4. In what ways have you experienced God's forgiveness in your own life, and how does this motivate you to extend forgiveness to others?

5. Think about a time that anger was your reaction to a situation and how you could have reacted differently. What would have been the difference? Are you still angry about that time?

154

Week 39: Zacchaeus: A Story of Transformation

The story of Zacchaeus is a narrative of redemption and transformation. Despite his reputation as a tax collector and outsider, Zacchaeus encountered Jesus and experienced a radical change in his heart and life. Tax collectors in those days were known as cheats and liars – they were able to cheat people with no consequences.   Let's explore the life of Zacchaeus, examining his strengths, weaknesses, and the ways in which God used him for His glory.

Verse to Review: Luke 19:10

"For the Son of Man came to seek and to save the lost."

History of Zacchaeus:

Zacchaeus was a chief tax collector in Jericho, a position that often earned him scorn and contempt from his fellow Jews. As a collaborator with the oppressive Roman authorities, Zacchaeus was viewed as a traitor and sinner by his own people. Despite his wealth and social status, Zacchaeus felt a deep sense of emptiness and longing for something more.

Zacchaeus's Strengths and Flaws:

Zacchaeus's greatest strength was his willingness to seek out Jesus, despite the obstacles that stood in his way. Despite his short stature and the crowds that surrounded Jesus, Zacchaeus climbed a sycamore-fig tree to catch a glimpse of the Messiah. However, Zacchaeus also had his flaws, particularly his involvement in unethical practices as a tax collector. His profession led to widespread resentment and condemnation from the Jewish community.

As a tax collector, Zacchaeus was known for exploiting his fellow Jews by collecting more taxes than required and pocketing the excess for personal gain. His actions not only fueled resentment and anger among the people but also contributed to his reputation as a sinner and outcast in society.

Despite his wealth and status, Zacchaeus likely faced significant pressure from Roman authorities to fulfill his duties as a tax collector. While this does not excuse his unethical behavior, it highlights the complex social and political dynamics at play during that time. Zacchaeus's decision to prioritize worldly wealth and status over integrity and righteousness ultimately led to spiritual emptiness and dissatisfaction.

Zacchaeus's occupation as a tax collector isolated him from his own community, leading to feelings of loneliness and alienation. Zacchaeus likely longed for acceptance and belonging, yet found himself ostracized and marginalized by his fellow Jews.

God's Redemption Through Zacchaeus's Faith:

Brand 316 Inc www.brand316.org 727 North Waco #290 Wichita KS 67203 (316) 247-2050

Despite Zacchaeus's flaws and shortcomings, Jesus saw beyond his outward appearance and recognized the potential for transformation within him. When Jesus called out to Zacchaeus and invited Himself to his home, Zacchaeus responded with joy and repentance. In a dramatic display of transformation, Zacchaeus pledged to give half of his possessions to the poor and repay four times the amount to anyone he had cheated. As a Christian we are expected to live our life focused on honoring Christ.

Conclusion:

Zacchaeus's encounter with Jesus serves as a powerful illustration of the transformative power of grace and forgiveness. Despite his past mistakes and failures, Zacchaeus experienced God's unconditional love and acceptance through Jesus's invitation to dine with him. This encounter not only brought about a profound change in Zacchaeus's heart and life but also served as a catalyst for reconciliation and restoration within the community.

One of the most remarkable aspects of Zacchaeus's story is his willingness to respond to Jesus's call with repentance and obedience. Despite his wealth and social status, Zacchaeus recognized the emptiness and futility of his pursuit of worldly gain and willingly surrendered everything to follow Jesus. His act of generosity and restitution demonstrated a genuine transformation of heart and a desire to make amends for past wrongs. Can you think of a story in the Bible where someone chose a different path?

Zacchaeus's story also serves as a powerful reminder of the importance of seeking out Jesus with sincerity and humility. Despite the obstacles and challenges that stood in his way, he was willing to climb a tree to catch a glimpse of the Messiah. His determination and persistence paid off when Jesus not only noticed him but also invited Himself to Zacchaeus's home. This act of grace and acceptance not only transformed Zacchaeus's life but also served as a testimony to the transformative power of encountering Jesus.

Jesus stands ready to forgive and transform us. Pray and trust in Him - respond with joy and obedience to Jesus's call, surrendering everything to follow Him wholeheartedly.

Zacchaeus's story is a powerful reminder of God's redemptive power and His ability to transform even the most unlikely people. Despite his flaws and shortcomings, Zacchaeus encountered Jesus and experienced a radical change in his heart and life. As we reflect on his story, be encouraged to seek out Jesus with sincerity and repentance, knowing that He stands ready to forgive and transform us.

Reflective Questions - Answer In Writing

1. In what ways do Zacchaeus's flaws and shortcomings resonate with your own struggles and challenges?

2. Reflect on a time when you experienced rejection or isolation. How did that experience impact your relationship with God and others?

3. Consider Zacchaeus's response to Jesus's invitation. How can we cultivate a similar spirit of repentance and transformation in our own lives?

4. Despite his past mistakes, Zacchaeus encountered Jesus and experienced a radical change in his heart and life. How does this give you hope for your own journey of faith?

5. How can you emulate Zacchaeus's example of seeking out Jesus with sincerity and repentance in your own life?

James 1:22 is a verse that challenges Christians to not only hear God's Word but to act on it. It's a call to live out our faith in practical ways. This study will explore the meaning of this verse, its context, and how we can apply it to our daily lives.

The Book of James

The Book of James, written by James, the brother of Jesus, is known for its practical wisdom. It addresses real-life issues and encourages believers to live out their faith in tangible ways. James emphasizes the importance of faith in action, reminding Christians that true faith results in good deeds.

Immediate Context

James 1:22 is part of a passage where James talks about listening to and doing the Word. In the verses leading up to James 1:22, he encourages believers to be quick to listen, slow to speak, and slow to become angry (James 1:19). He also emphasizes the importance of getting rid of moral filth and humbly accepting the Word planted in us (James 1:21).

Exploring James 1:22

The Text

"Do not merely listen to the word, and so deceive yourselves. Do what it says" (James 1:22, NIV).

Key Phrases

1. **"Do not merely listen to the word"**

   o This phrase warns against being passive listeners. It's not enough to just hear God's Word; we need to engage with it.

2. **"And so deceive yourselves"**

   o This implies that if we only listen and don't act, we are fooling ourselves. We might think we're being faithful, but we're missing the point.

3. **"Do what it says"**

   o The call to action. We must put God's Word into practice in our daily lives.

Theological Implications

Active Faith

James 1:22 highlights the importance of active faith. It's not enough to just know what the Bible says; we need to live it out. This active faith shows that we truly believe and trust in God's Word.

Self-Deception

The verse warns against self-deception. It's easy to think we're being faithful by simply listening to sermons or reading the Bible, but if our actions don't reflect what we've learned, we're deceiving ourselves.

Obedience

True faith requires obedience. Doing what God's Word says is a way of showing our love and commitment to Him. It's about aligning our lives with His will and purpose.

Practical Applications

Listening and Acting

We need to be more than just listeners. This means taking what we hear and read in the Bible and applying it to our lives. For example, if the Bible teaches us to love our neighbors, we should actively look for ways to show love and kindness to those around us. That is true in every situation you are in – now and in the future!

Regular Self-Examination

Regularly examining our lives helps ensure we're not just hearing the Word but living it. This involves reflecting on our actions and attitudes and asking if they align with God's teachings.

Accountability

Having someone to hold us accountable can help us live out our faith. This could be a friend, mentor, or small group who encourages us and challenges us to apply God's Word in our lives.

Misunderstandings and Cautions

Hearing vs. Doing

Some people think that just hearing the Word is enough. However, James 1:22 makes it clear that we must also do what it says. True faith is shown through our actions.

Legalism

We must be careful not to fall into legalism, where we focus only on actions and miss the heart behind them. Our obedience should come from a genuine love for God and a desire to follow Him, not from a sense of obligation or to earn favor.

Brand 316 Inc www.brand316.org 727 North Waco #290 Wichita KS 67203 (316) 247-2050

Selective Obedience

It's easy to pick and choose which parts of the Bible we want to follow. However, James 1:22 calls us to obey all of God's Word, not just the parts that are convenient or easy.

Biblical Examples

The Good Samaritan

The story of the Good Samaritan (Luke 10:25-37) is a great example of James 1:22 in action. The Samaritan didn't just hear about loving his neighbor; he acted on it by helping a wounded man, even when others passed by. This story shows the importance of putting love into action.

Jesus' Teaching on the Wise and Foolish Builders

In Matthew 7:24-27, Jesus talks about the wise and foolish builders. The wise builder hears Jesus' words and puts them into practice, building his house on a rock. The foolish builder hears but doesn't act, building on sand. When storms come, only the house on the rock stands. This parable illustrates the importance of doing what Jesus says.

Conclusion

James 1:22 is a powerful reminder that true faith involves action. It's not enough to just listen to God's Word; we need to live it out in our daily lives. By understanding the context, meaning, and practical applications of this verse, we can grow in our faith and live out God's teachings more fully.

As Christians, we are called to be doers of the Word, not just hearers. This involves actively applying God's teachings, examining our lives, and holding ourselves accountable. By doing so, we show our love and commitment to God and reflect His love to those around us. Let's strive to be people who not only hear God's Word but also live it out in every aspect of our lives.

Reflective Questions - Answer in Writing

1. How does James 1:22 challenge your understanding of obedience and faithfulness in response to God's Word?

2. Reflect on a time when you heard the Word of God but struggled to put it into practice. What barriers or obstacles prevented you from obeying God's Word?

3. In what areas do you need to be more intentional about applying God's Word to your life?

4. Reflect on the concept of spiritual deception and self-delusion. How can you guard against self-deception and ensure that your faith is genuine and authentic?

5. How does James 1:22 inspire you to live out your faith in practical ways, demonstrating obedience and integrity in all areas of your life?

Week 41: King Solomon: Wisdom, Wealth, and Waywardness

King Solomon, renowned for his wisdom and wealth, is a central figure in the Old Testament known for his profound insights, lavish lifestyle, and eventual spiritual decline. His story serves as a cautionary tale about the dangers of straying from God's commands and the consequences of pursuing earthly pleasures and wisdom apart from God. In this lesson, we will explore the life of King Solomon, examining his strengths, weaknesses, and the valuable lessons we can learn from his successes and failures.

Verse to Review: 1 Kings 3:9

"So give your servant a discerning heart to govern your people and to distinguish between right and wrong. For who is able to govern this great people of yours?"

Background of King Solomon:

King Solomon was the son of King David and Bathsheba, chosen by God to succeed his father as king of Israel. He ascended to the throne at a young age and was granted wisdom and discernment by God in response to his humble request. Under Solomon's reign, Israel experienced unprecedented prosperity and peace, marked by economic growth, cultural development, and the construction of the magnificent Temple in Jerusalem. However, despite his initial devotion to God and wisdom in governance, Solomon's later years were marred by spiritual compromise, idolatry, and disobedience.

Strengths and Flaws of King Solomon:

King Solomon possessed both strengths and weaknesses that shaped his reign and legacy. Some of his strengths include:

1. **Wisdom and Discernment:** Solomon was renowned for his unparalleled wisdom and discernment, which he demonstrated in his judgments, proverbs, and writings. His request for wisdom to govern God's people reflects his humility and desire to lead with integrity and righteousness. He was a man of wisdom and a man of foolishness.
2. **Wealth and Prosperity:** Under Solomon's rule, Israel experienced unprecedented wealth and prosperity, fueled by trade, tribute, and taxation. His economic policies and diplomatic alliances contributed to Israel's rise as a regional power and center of commerce and culture.
3. **Architectural and Cultural Achievements:** Solomon's reign was characterized by remarkable architectural and cultural achievements, including the construction of the Temple in Jerusalem, the expansion of the royal palace, and the promotion of trade and cultural exchange with neighboring nations.

Flaws and weaknesses:

1. **Idolatry:** Despite being blessed with wisdom and wealth by God, Solomon's downfall was his propensity towards idolatry. He married many foreign wives, including daughters of pagan kings, who influenced him to worship their gods (1 Kings 11:1-8). Solomon allowed these wives to build altars and temples to their gods within Jerusalem, violating God's commandment to worship Him alone. His idolatrous practices were a betrayal of the covenant between God and Israel and led to divine judgment upon Solomon's kingdom, resulting in its eventual division after his death.

2. **Multiplication of Wives and Concubines:** Despite God's explicit command for kings not to multiply wives unto themselves (Deuteronomy 17:17), Solomon disregarded this instruction and accumulated a vast harem of wives and concubines. His pursuit of numerous marriages was likely motivated by political alliances and desires for personal gratification rather than obedience to God's law. Solomon's relationships with these women, many of whom were from pagan nations, contributed to his eventual turn towards idolatry as they influenced him to worship foreign gods. His disregard for God's commandments regarding marriage weakened his spiritual foundation and led to the erosion of his fidelity to God.

3. **Worldly Wisdom Over Spiritual Discernment:** While Solomon was renowned for his wisdom, his reliance on worldly wisdom sometimes overshadowed his need for spiritual discernment. Instead of seeking God's guidance in all matters, Solomon sometimes relied solely on his own intellect and understanding. This lack of dependence on God's wisdom led him to make decisions that were not aligned with God's will, ultimately contributing to his spiritual downfall (1 Kings 11:1-13).

4. **Injustice and Oppression:** Despite being called to uphold justice and righteousness as a king of Israel, Solomon's reign was marked by instances of injustice and oppression. His policies, such as forced labor and heavy taxation, burdened the people of Israel and led to widespread dissatisfaction (1 Kings 12:4). Solomon's failure to ensure fairness and equity among his subjects weakened the social fabric of his kingdom and undermined the principles of justice that God had established.

5. **Failure to Pass on Faith:** Despite Solomon's personal faith and relationship with God, he did not adequately pass on his faith to the next generation. His failure to instill a strong foundation of faith in his successors left the kingdom vulnerable to spiritual decline and eventual division. Instead of prioritizing the spiritual upbringing of his children and heirs, Solomon's focus on his own legacy and achievements resulted in a lack of continuity in the spiritual leadership of Israel, contributing to its eventual downfall (1 Kings 11:9-13).

God's Response to King Solomon:

God remained faithful to His covenant with David and continued to extend mercy and grace to Israel. He rose up prophets to warn Solomon of the consequences of his disobedience and called him to repentance and renewal. Although Solomon's reign ended in disappointment and division, God preserved a remnant of faithful believers and continued to work out His purposes in the midst of human frailty and failure.

The story of King Solomon serves as a reminder about the dangers of compromising with sin and pursuing worldly wisdom and pleasures apart from God. Solomon's wisdom and wealth, while impressive, ultimately proved to be insufficient to satisfy the deepest longings of the human heart. Only a relationship with God founded on humility, obedience, and trust can bring true fulfillment and joy.

Conclusion:

King Solomon's story continues to resonate with believers today, serving as a reminder of the consequences of compromising with sin and pursuing worldly pleasures and wisdom apart from God. In a culture that often values material success, intellectual achievement, and self-gratification above all else, Solomon's life serves as a cautionary tale about the emptiness and futility of such pursuits when divorced from a vibrant relationship with God. Without God, life is empty.

Moreover, King Solomon's story challenges us to examine our own hearts and priorities in light of God's Word and His will for our lives. Are we seeking wisdom and guidance from God through prayer, Scripture, and the counsel of wise mentors and fellow believers, or are we relying solely on our own understanding and abilities? Are we using the resources and opportunities God has entrusted to us for His glory and the advancement of His kingdom, or are we squandering them on selfish pursuits and temporal pleasures?

King Solomon's story invites us to consider the legacy we are leaving behind for future generations. Despite Solomon's many accomplishments and contributions to Israel's prosperity and cultural development, his reign ended in disappointment and division due to his spiritual compromise and disobedience. As followers of Christ, we are called to live lives marked by faithfulness, integrity, and obedience to God's commands, knowing that our choices and actions have far-reaching consequences beyond our own lifetimes. We should desire leaving this world knowing that we have spread the word of Christ and helped other meet Him personally.

In conclusion, the story of King Solomon challenges us to prioritize spiritual growth, righteousness, and obedience in our relationship with God and others. His successes and failures serve as a sobering reminder of the fleeting nature of earthly wealth and pleasures and the enduring value of a life lived in accordance with God's commands. As we reflect on Solomon's story, may we be inspired to seek wisdom, righteousness, and faithfulness in all areas of our lives, trusting in God's grace and guidance to lead us on the path of abundant life and eternal significance.

Reflective Questions - Answer in Writing

1. In what ways do you see yourself in the strengths and weaknesses of King Solomon?

2. Reflect on a time when you prioritized earthly wisdom or pleasures over seeking God's wisdom and will. How did this impact your relationship with God and others?

3. Consider the importance of humility and obedience in Solomon's request for wisdom. How can we cultivate a similar attitude of humility and dependence on God in our own lives?

4. Reflect on Solomon's pursuit of pleasure and luxury. How can we guard against the allure of worldly riches and pleasures and instead seek fulfillment in God alone?

5. How does the story of King Solomon challenge you to prioritize spiritual growth, righteousness, and obedience in your relationship with God and others?

Romans 8:28 is one of the most cherished and frequently quoted verses in the Bible. It offers profound reassurance and hope to believers, reminding them of God's sovereignty and His active role in their lives. However, the depth and implications of this verse can often be misunderstood or oversimplified. This study will delve into the context, meaning, and application of Romans 8:28, aiming to provide a comprehensive understanding of how God works all things for the good of those who love Him and are called according to His purpose.

Context of Romans 8:28

The Book of Romans

The Book of Romans, written by the Apostle Paul addresses important Christian principles and practical living. Romans 8 stands out as a chapter of assurance, beginning with the declaration that "there is now no condemnation for those who are in Christ Jesus" (Romans 8:1) and ending with the promise that nothing can separate believers from the love of God (Romans 8:38-39).

Immediate Context

Romans 8:28 comes in a part of the chapter where Paul talks about the role of the Holy Spirit in our lives. He mentions the suffering we experience now and the glory that will come later. The verses before Romans 8:28 talk about how the Holy Spirit helps us pray and aligns our prayers with God's will.

Exploring Romans 8:28

The Text

"And we know that in all things God works for the good of those who love him, who have been called according to his purpose" (Romans 8:28, NIV).

Key Phrases

1. **"And we know"**

   o   This phrase signifies certainty and assurance. Paul is expressing a truth that believers can confidently hold on to.

2. **"In all things"**

   o   This encompasses every aspect of life, including both the good and the bad. It indicates that there is no situation beyond God's sovereign control.

3. **"God works for the good"**

Brand 316 Inc   www.brand316.org 727 North Waco #290 Wichita KS 67203 (316) 247-2050

- God's active involvement in orchestrating events for the ultimate good of believers. This does not mean that everything that happens is good, but that God can bring good out of every situation.

4. **"Those who love him"**

- This refers to believers, those who have a personal relationship with God and who are committed to loving Him.

5. **"Who have been called according to his purpose"**

- This highlights God's calling and purpose for believers. It indicates that God's plan is intentional and purposeful.

Theological Implications

God's Sovereignty

Romans 8:28 underscores the sovereignty of God. He is in control of all circumstances, working behind the scenes to bring about His divine purposes. This promise of God's sovereignty provides comfort and hope, especially in times of suffering and uncertainty.

The Good God Works

The "good" that God works towards is not necessarily immediate comfort or happiness but conforms to His ultimate purpose. This includes spiritual growth, character development, and ultimately, our conformity to the image of Christ (Romans 8:29). This perspective helps believers trust in God's plan, even when situations do not make sense.

The Role of Believers

While God's sovereignty is central, the verse also emphasizes the relationship believers have with Him. Those who love God and are called according to His purpose can trust in His promise to work all things for their good. This relationship is marked by love, trust, and a commitment to God's purposes.

Practical Applications

Trusting God's Plan

Believers are called to trust in God's plan, even when it is not immediately clear or when circumstances are challenging. This trust is rooted in the assurance that God is sovereign and good.

Perseverance in Trials

Romans 8:28 encourages believers to endure through trials, knowing that God can bring good out of even the most difficult situations. This perspective can transform how believers view suffering, seeing it as an opportunity for growth and reliance on God.

Loving God and Aligning with His Purpose

The verse calls believers to love God and align their lives with His purpose. This involves seeking God's will, living according to His Word, and being open to the Spirit's leading.

Misunderstandings and Cautions

Over-Simplification

Romans 8:28 is sometimes misunderstood as a promise that everything will turn out positively in the short term. However, the "good" that God works towards is often part of a larger, eternal perspective that may not be immediately evident.

Ignoring Context

Taking this verse out of context can lead to a misunderstanding. It is crucial to consider the surrounding passages that speak to the reality of suffering and the role of the Holy Spirit in interceding for believers.

Seeking Verses to Fit Personal Desires

We must be cautious not to use this verse to justify personal desires or decisions without seeking a broader understanding of God's will. It is important to approach Scripture with a heart open to God's teaching, rather than trying to fit God's Word into preconceived notions.

Biblical Examples

Joseph's Story

Joseph's life, as recounted in Genesis, is a powerful illustration of Romans 8:28. Despite being sold into slavery, falsely accused, and imprisoned, Joseph remained faithful to God. Eventually, God used these circumstances to elevate Joseph to a position where he could save many lives during a famine. Joseph himself acknowledged God's sovereignty, saying to his brothers, "You intended to harm me, but God intended it for good to accomplish what is now being done, the saving of many lives" (Genesis 50:20, NIV).

Paul's Ministry

The Apostle Paul experienced numerous hardships, including imprisonment, beatings, and shipwrecks. Yet, he remained steadfast in his mission, trusting that God was at work in all circumstances. In his letter to the Philippians, Paul writes, "Now I want you to know, brothers and sisters, that what has happened to me has actually served to advance the gospel" (Philippians 1:12, NIV). Paul's trials contributed to the spread of the gospel and the strengthening of the early church.

Conclusion

Romans 8:28 is a powerful promise that God is always at work in our lives, using everything for our ultimate good. This assurance is based on God's control, His definition of "good," and our relationship with Him. By understanding the context, meaning, and application of this verse, we can face life's challenges with confidence and hope.

As Christians, we are called to trust God's plan, persevere through tough times, and align our lives with His purpose. While it's important to avoid misunderstandings, the promise of Romans 8:28 remains a source of great encouragement. No matter what happens, we can be sure that God is at work, bringing about His good purposes for those who love Him and are called according to His purpose.

Reflective Questions - Answer in Writing

1. How does Romans 8:28 speak to your understanding of God's providence and sovereignty?

2. Reflect on a time when you experienced God's faithfulness in working all things together for good. What did this experience teach you about God's character?

3. How does your love for God influence your perspective on life's challenges?

4. In what areas of your life do you need to surrender to God's sovereign will, trusting that He knows what is best for you?

5. How can you develop an attitude of thankfulness and praise, even in trials and difficulties?

Week 43: Rahab: A Prostitute to Salvation

The story of Rahab is a testament to the power of faith and redemption. Despite her past as a prostitute and outsider, Rahab played a crucial role in the story of Israel's conquest of Jericho and ultimately became part of the lineage of Jesus Christ. In this lesson, we will explore the life of Rahab, examining her strengths, weaknesses, and the ways in which God used her for His glory.

Verse to Review: Hebrews 11:31

"By faith the prostitute Rahab, because she welcomed the spies, was not killed with those who were disobedient."

History of Rahab:

Rahab was a Canaanite woman who lived in the city of Jericho at the time of Israel's conquest of the land. Despite her status as an outsider and her occupation as a prostitute, Rahab demonstrated remarkable courage and faith when she sheltered Israelite spies sent to gather information about the city. Rahab's actions not only saved the lives of the spies but also secured her own salvation and the salvation of her family by giving her a second chance in life.

Rahab's Strengths and Flaws:

Rahab's greatest strength was her unwavering faith in the God of Israel. Despite being surrounded by a culture steeped in idolatry and immorality, Rahab recognized the power and sovereignty of the Israelite God and chose to align herself with His people. Rahab's willingness to risk her own life to protect the spies and her subsequent conversion to the faith of Israel demonstrate her courage and conviction. However, Rahab also had her flaws, including her involvement in the sinful practices of her culture and her past as a prostitute.

As a prostitute in the city of Jericho, Rahab was involved in the sinful practices of her culture, including idolatry and immorality. Despite her upbringing and environment, Rahab recognized the emptiness of her way of life and chose to align herself with the God of Israel. Rahab's past as a prostitute likely carried a significant stigma in the eyes of her fellow Israelites. Despite her courageous actions in protecting the spies and her subsequent conversion to the faith of Israel, Rahab may have faced judgment and condemnation from others due to her past.

By sheltering the Israelite spies and aiding in their escape from Jericho, Rahab risked her own life and the lives of her family members. Rahab's actions required great courage and faith, as she chose to fear and trust in the God of Israel rather than the rulers of Jericho.

God's Redemption Through Rahab's Faith:

Despite Rahab's past and her status as an outsider, God demonstrated His grace and mercy towards her by including her in the lineage of Jesus Christ (Matthew 15 & she married Salmon of the Tribe of Judah and was the mother of Boaz). Rahab's courageous actions in protecting the Israelite spies and her subsequent conversion to the faith of Israel serve as a powerful testimony to God's ability to transform lives and use unlikely individuals for His purposes.

Conclusion:

Rahab's story is a powerful reminder of God's ability to redeem and transform even the most unlikely people for His purposes. Time after time, God uses our past failures for His glory – that will be true with you also. Despite her past as a prostitute and outsider, Rahab's courageous actions in protecting the Israelite spies and aligning herself with the God of Israel demonstrated her faith and conviction. Rahab's inclusion in the lineage of Jesus Christ highlights God's grace and mercy towards all who come to Him in faith.

One of the most striking aspects of Rahab's story is her willingness to risk everything for the sake of her faith. Despite the dangers involved, Rahab chose to trust/fear in the God of Israel rather than the rulers of Jericho. Her courageous actions not only saved the lives of the Israelite spies but also secured her own salvation and the salvation of her family. Rahab's story challenges us to examine our own commitment to our faith and willingness to take risks for the sake of God's kingdom.

Rahab's story also serves as a powerful example of God's grace and mercy towards those who may have experienced rejection or judgment from others. Despite her past as a prostitute and the stigma she likely faced, God saw beyond Rahab's outward appearance and recognized her faith and courage.

Rahab's story is a powerful reminder of God's grace and the transformative power of faith. Despite her past as a prostitute and outsider, Rahab demonstrated remarkable courage and faith when she sheltered the Israelite spies and aligned herself with the God of Israel. As we reflect on Rahab's story, may we be challenged to examine our own hearts and lives before God. May we, like Rahab, choose to trust in God's grace and mercy, knowing that He is able to redeem and transform even the most unlikely people for His purpose.

Reflective Questions - Answer in Writing

1. In what ways do Rahab's strengths and weaknesses resonate with your own experiences and struggles?

2. Reflect on a time when you had to take a courageous stand for your faith, despite the risks involved. How did God honor your faithfulness?

3. Consider Rahab's past as a prostitute and the stigma she likely faced. How can we show grace and compassion towards those who have experienced similar struggles?

4. Despite her past, God used Rahab to play a crucial role in the story of Israel's conquest of Jericho and ultimately included her in the lineage of Jesus Christ. How does Rahab's story give you hope for your own journey of faith and redemption?

5. How can you cultivate a spirit of courage and faith, like Rahab, in your own relationship with God?

Week 44: James 5:16 - The Power of Confession and Prayer

James 5:16 highlights the importance of confession, prayer, and mutual support among believers. It reviews the power of prayer and the healing that comes from genuine confession and intercession. Throughout the Bible we learn how powerful prayer is for our lives and those we pray for. As Christians, we have a direct line to God – a God that cares for and loves us. Prayer needs to be a major part of your daily life.

The Book of James

The Book of James is a practical epistle written by James, the brother of Jesus. It addresses various aspects of Christian living, emphasizing the importance of faith being demonstrated through actions. James covers topics such as perseverance, wisdom, speech, and community relationships.

Immediate Context

James 5:13-20 focuses on the power of prayer, the importance of mutual confession, and the need for intercession. James encourages believers to pray in all circumstances—whether in trouble, happy, or sick. He emphasizes the role of community in providing support, healing, and encouragement through prayer.

Exploring James 5:16

The Text

"Therefore confess your sins to each other and pray for each other so that you may be healed. The prayer of a righteous person is powerful and effective" (James 5:16, NIV).

Key Phrases

1. **"Therefore confess your sins to each other"**

   o This encourages Christians to openly acknowledge their sins to one another, fostering honesty, accountability, and mutual support within the community.

2. **"And pray for each other so that you may be healed"**

   o This highlights the importance of prayer, where believers pray for one another's needs, leading to physical, emotional, and spiritual healing.

3. **"The prayer of a righteous person is powerful and effective"**

   o This affirms the strength and impact of the prayers of those who live righteously, emphasizing the importance of living in accordance with God's will.

173

Brand 316 Inc www.brand316.org 727 North Waco #290 Wichita KS 67203 (316) 247-2050

Theological Implications

The Power of Confession

Confession is an integral part of Christian living. It brings hidden sins into the light, enabling healing and restoration. Confession to one another fosters a sense of community and accountability, strengthening the body of Christ.

The Role of Prayer

Prayer is a powerful tool for believers. It is a means of communicating with God, interceding for others, and seeking God's intervention. The effectiveness of prayer is tied to the righteousness of the one praying, highlighting the importance of a righteous life.

Mutual Support and Healing

James 5:16 emphasizes the communal aspect of the Christian faith. Mutual confession and prayer create a supportive environment where believers can experience healing and growth. This mutual support is essential for a healthy and thriving Christian community.

Practical Applications

Encouraging a Culture of Confession

Encourage a culture where confession is normalized. Create safe spaces within your church or small group where people can share their struggles and sins without fear of judgment. This openness creates trust and accountability.

Committing to Intercessory Prayer

Make intercessory prayer a regular practice. Dedicate time to pray for the needs of others, whether they are facing physical illness, emotional struggles, or spiritual battles. Believe in the power of your prayers and the impact they can have on others.

Living a Righteous Life

Strive to live a life that aligns with God's will. The effectiveness of your prayers is connected to your righteousness. Seek to obey God's commands, pursue holiness, and maintain a close relationship with Him.

Misunderstandings and Cautions

Confession and Privacy

While confession is important, it should be done wisely. Not every setting is appropriate for sharing deeply personal sins. Seek trusted and mature believers for confession, ensuring that it is done in a safe and confidential environment.

Misinterpreting Healing

Healing mentioned in James 5:16 can be physical, emotional, or spiritual. It is important not to limit the understanding of healing to physical ailments alone. Recognize that God works in various ways to bring about healing and restoration.

Balancing Righteousness and Grace

The emphasis on the prayer of a righteous person should not lead to self-righteousness or legalism. Remember that righteousness is a result of God's grace and our response to His love. It is not about earning God's favor but living in gratitude and obedience to Him.

Biblical Examples

Nehemiah's Prayer

Nehemiah 1:5-11 records Nehemiah's prayer of confession and intercession for the people of Israel. Nehemiah acknowledges the sins of the Israelites and seeks God's favor and guidance for the task ahead. His prayer demonstrates the power of intercessory prayer and the importance of seeking God's intervention in difficult circumstances.

The Early Church

Acts 2:42-47 describes the early church's commitment to prayer, fellowship, and mutual support. The believers shared their possessions, prayed together, and supported one another. This communal living and mutual care led to spiritual and numerical growth, showcasing the power of a prayerful and supportive community.

Conclusion

James 5:16 provides profound insights into the importance of confession, prayer, and mutual support within the Christian community. We should confess our sins to one another, pray for each other, and live righteously. By doing so, we experience the power of prayer and the healing that comes from genuine confession and intercession.

Reflective Questions – Answer in Writing

1. How can you create a safe and supportive environment for confession within your faith community?

2. What steps can you take to make prayer a regular practice in your life?

3. How does understanding the power of a righteous person's prayer influence your commitment to living a righteous life?

4. Reflect on a time when you experienced healing—physical, emotional, or spiritual—through the prayers of others. How did that impact your faith?

5. How can you encourage and support others to embrace the practices of confession and intercessory prayer?

Week 45: Sarah: Trusting in God's Promises

The story of Sarah, the wife of Abraham, is one of faith, doubt, and ultimately, God's faithfulness. Despite her moments of weakness and uncertainty, Sarah's life serves as a testament to the power of trusting in God's promises. In this lesson, we will jump into the life of Sarah, exploring her strengths, weaknesses, and the ways in which God used her for His glory.

Verse to Review: Genesis 18:14

"Is anything too hard for the Lord? I will return to you at the appointed time next year, and Sarah will have a son."

History of Sarah:

Sarah, originally named Sarai, was the wife of Abraham and played a crucial role in the fulfillment of God's promises to him. She journeyed alongside Abraham, facing numerous trials and challenges, including infertility and exile. Despite her initial doubt and disbelief, Sarah ultimately became the mother of Isaac, the child of promise, through whom the nation of Israel would be born.

Sarah's Strengths and Flaws:

Sarah's greatest strength lay in her unwavering loyalty to her husband and her willingness to follow him wherever God led. She supported Abraham through countless trials and remained steadfast in her commitment to him, even in the face of adversity.

However, Sarah also struggled with doubt and impatience, particularly when it came to God's promises of a son. In a moment of weakness, she laughed at the prospect of bearing a child in her old age, unable to comprehend the possibility of such a miracle (Genesis 18:12). Despite God's assurances, Sarah struggled to believe that she would conceive and bear a child in her old age. This lack of faith led her to laugh in disbelief when God reiterated His promise to Abraham. Sarah's doubt revealed a deeper struggle to trust in God's faithfulness, especially when faced with seemingly impossible circumstances.

She also attempted to work problems out on her own, without consulting God. Instead of waiting patiently for God's timing, Sarah took matters into her own hands and devised a plan to fulfill God's promise through her maidservant, Hagar. By offering Hagar to Abraham as a surrogate mother, Sarah sought to bypass God's plan and secure a son for herself (Genesis 16:1-3). This act of self-reliance demonstrated Sarah's impatience and her failure to trust in God's sovereignty.

When confronted about her laughter and disbelief, Sarah attempted to shift the blame onto Abraham, denying her own culpability (Genesis 18:15). Instead of owning up to her doubts and shortcomings, Sarah sought to deflect responsibility onto her husband, revealing a lack of humility and a failure to acknowledge her own faults.

God's Redemption Through Sarah's Faith:

Despite Sarah's doubts and disbelief, God remained faithful to His promise to her. He visited Abraham and Sarah, reaffirming His plan to bless them with a son in their old age. True to His word, Sarah conceived and bore Isaac, fulfilling the long-awaited promise of God (Genesis 21:1-7). Through Isaac, God continued to fulfill His covenant with Abraham, ensuring that his descendants would be as numerous as the stars in the sky and the sand on the seashore.

Conclusion:

Sarah's journey of faith is a testament to the transformative power of God's promises in the lives of His people. From her initial incredulity at the prospect of bearing a child in her old age to the fulfillment of that promise in the birth of Isaac, Sarah's story is a powerful reminder that nothing is too difficult for the Lord. Despite her doubts and fears, God remained faithful to His word, proving time and again that His plans cannot be thwarted by human frailty or disbelief.

One of the most striking aspects of Sarah's story is the way in which God used her weaknesses and shortcomings to bring about His purposes. Despite her advanced age and physical limitations, God chose Sarah to be the mother of the promised child, Isaac, through whom the covenant blessings would be fulfilled. In doing so, God demonstrated His sovereignty and power, showing that He is able to accomplish His will through even the most unlikely vessels.

As we reflect on Sarah's story, we are challenged to examine our own lives and consider the ways in which God is calling us to trust in His promises. Like Sarah, we may face moments of doubt and uncertainty, but we can take comfort in the knowledge that God is faithful and His plans for us are good.

Sarah's flaws serve as a reminder that even the most faithful are prone to moments of weakness and doubt. Like Sarah, we may struggle to fully trust in God's promises, especially when faced with difficult circumstances or prolonged waiting periods. However, Sarah's story also demonstrates that God is gracious and patient with His people, even when they falter in their faith. He is able to work through our weaknesses and doubts to bring about His purposes, ultimately bringing glory to His name.

In Sarah's attempt to work out her problems on her own, we see the danger of relying on our own understanding and abilities rather than seeking God's guidance and wisdom. Despite her best intentions, Sarah's decision to give Hagar to Abraham as a surrogate mother only led to further complications and strife within her household. It was only when Sarah turned to God in humility and dependence that He intervened and fulfilled His promise to her.

Finally, Sarah's tendency to blame others for her faults serves as a cautionary tale about the dangers of pride and self-righteousness. Instead of taking responsibility for her own actions, Sarah sought to shift the blame onto Abraham, denying her own culpability in the situation. In doing so, Sarah missed an opportunity for growth and repentance, choosing instead to preserve her own pride and reputation.

Sarah's story is a powerful reminder of the importance of trusting in God's promises, even in the face of doubt and uncertainty.

Sarah's life is a testament to the power of trusting in God's promises, even in the face of doubt and uncertainty. Despite her flaws and shortcomings, God used Sarah to bring about His purposes and fulfill His plans. As we reflect on Sarah's story, may we be encouraged to trust in God's faithfulness, knowing that He is able to accomplish far more than we could ask or imagine.

Reflective Questions - Answer in Writing

1. In what areas of your life do you struggle with doubt and disbelief, like Sarah did?

2. Reflect on a time when God proved Himself faithful to you, despite your doubts and fears. How did that experience impact your faith?

3. Consider the consequences of Sarah's laughter and doubt. How can we learn from her example in our own walk with God?

4. Can you think of situations you are in right now that you should turn over completely to God?

5. How can you cultivate a deeper sense of trust in God's promises, even when circumstances seem bleak or impossible?

Week 46: Mark 2:17 - Calling Sinners to Repentance

Mark 2:17 reveals Jesus' mission and His heart for those who are spiritually and morally lost. This verse underscores the purpose of Christ's ministry—to call sinners to repentance and to offer them healing and transformation. As we review this verse, consider your life and your flaws (we all have them) and seriously consider the impact of this verse on your future.

The Gospel of Mark

The Gospel of Mark is believed to be the earliest of the four Gospels, written by John Mark. It presents a vivid and action-packed account of Jesus' life, ministry, death, and resurrection. Mark emphasizes Jesus' authority, His role as the suffering servant, and His mission to bring the kingdom of God to earth.

Immediate Context

Mark 2:17 is part of a narrative where Jesus is dining at the house of Levi (also known as Matthew), a tax collector. Tax collectors were despised by Jewish society for partnering with the Roman occupiers and often taking advantage of their fellow Jews. When the Pharisees, the religious leaders of the time, saw Jesus eating with tax collectors and sinners, they questioned His disciples about His choice of company. Jesus responds with the profound statement found in Mark 2:17.

Exploring Mark 2:17

The Text

"On hearing this, Jesus said to them, 'It is not the healthy who need a doctor, but the sick. I have not come to call the righteous, but sinners'" (Mark 2:17, NIV).

Key Phrases

1. **"It is not the healthy who need a doctor, but the sick"**

   o Jesus uses a common-sense analogy to explain His mission. Just as a doctor is needed for those who are ill, Jesus is needed by those who recognize their spiritual sickness and need for healing.

2. **"I have not come to call the righteous"**

   o Jesus contrasts the self-righteous with those who are aware of their sinfulness. The "righteous" in this context refers to those who believe they are morally superior and do not need repentance.

3. **"But sinners"**

- o Jesus' mission is to reach out to sinners—those who are aware of their failures, mistakes, and need for God's mercy. He calls them to repentance and offers them a new life.

Theological Implications

Jesus' Mission

Mark 2:17 clearly communicates Jesus' mission to seek and save the lost. His primary purpose is to call sinners to repentance and offer them the hope of transformation and eternal life.

The Need for Humility

The verse highlights the importance of recognizing one's own sinfulness and need for God's grace. Self-righteousness and pride can prevent you from experiencing the healing and salvation that Jesus offers.

God's Inclusive Love

Jesus' willingness to associate with tax collectors and sinners demonstrates God's inclusive love and grace. **No one is beyond the reach of God's mercy**, regardless of their past or societal status.

Practical Applications

Embracing Jesus' Call

Recognize and admit your own spiritual need. Jesus' call is for everyone who acknowledges their sinfulness and desires transformation. Embrace His invitation to repentance and new life.

Extending Grace to Others

Follow Jesus' example by reaching out to those who are disregarded, judged, or considered "sinners" by society. Show them the love, acceptance, and grace that Jesus extends to all.

Avoiding Self-Righteousness

Guard against self-righteous attitudes. Remember that everyone is in need of God's grace and that no one is superior to another in the eyes of God. Humility is key to experiencing and sharing God's love.

Misunderstandings and Cautions

Misinterpreting "Righteous"

Jesus' reference to the "righteous" is not an endorsement of their self-perceived righteousness. Rather, it is a critique of those who are blind to their own need for repentance and grace.

Avoiding Holiness

While Jesus associated with sinners, He did not condone sin. His goal was always repentance and transformation. Believers are called to love and engage with sinners while maintaining staying true to God.

Neglecting Personal Repentance

Jesus' call to sinners includes each of us. It is crucial to continually examine our own lives, repent of our sins, and seek God's forgiveness and transformation.

Biblical Examples

The Woman Caught in Adultery

In John 8:1-11, Jesus demonstrates His mission to call sinners to repentance. When a woman caught in adultery is brought to Him, He shows her mercy and challenges her accusers. He then tells her to "go and sin no more," emphasizing both grace and the call to transformation.

Zacchaeus the Tax Collector

In Luke 19:1-10, Jesus encounters Zacchaeus, a tax collector. Despite his societal status and sinful past, Zacchaeus experiences Jesus' transformative love. He repents and makes restitution, demonstrating the change that Jesus brings to a repentant heart.

The Prodigal Son

The parable of the Prodigal Son (Luke 15:11-32) illustrates God's heart for the lost. The younger son, who squanders his inheritance, is welcomed back by his father with open arms when he repents. **This story highlights the joy in heaven over one sinner who repents.**

Conclusion

Mark 2:17 provides a profound insight into Jesus' mission and heart for the lost. We are called to recognize our own need for repentance, embrace Jesus' invitation to new life, and extend His grace to those around us. By doing so, we fulfill our calling to be His disciples and reflect His love to a world in need. We all fall short of the Glory of God!

Reflective Questions – Answer in Writing

1. How does recognizing your own spiritual need impact your relationship with Jesus?

2. In what ways can you reach out to those who are marginalized or judged by society, showing them the love of Christ? (think about where you are)

3. How can you maintain humility in your walk with God?

4. Reflect on a time when you experienced God's grace and transformation. How can you share that experience with others?

5. What steps (habits) can you take to continually examine your life, repent of your sins, and seek God's forgiveness and transformation?

Week 47: Aaron: The High Priest and the Golden Calf

Aaron, the older brother of Moses, played a significant role in the exodus of the Israelites from Egypt and the establishment of the priesthood in ancient Israel. While he was chosen by God to serve as the first high priest, Aaron's life also includes moments of triumph and failure, obedience and disobedience. In this lesson, we will explore the life of Aaron, examining his strengths, weaknesses, and the valuable lessons we can learn from his experiences.

Verse to Review: Exodus 28:1

"Have Aaron your brother brought to you from among the Israelites, along with his sons Nadab and Abihu, Eleazar and Ithamar, so they may serve me as priests."

Background of Aaron:

Aaron was born into the tribe of Levi during the time of Israel's enslavement in Egypt. He was chosen by God, along with his brother Moses, to confront Pharaoh and demand the release of the Israelites. Despite initial reluctance, Aaron eventually became Moses' spokesperson and played a central role in the miraculous deliverance of the Israelites from bondage. Following their exodus from Egypt, Aaron was consecrated as the first high priest of Israel, responsible for overseeing the tabernacle worship and offering sacrifices on behalf of the people.

Strengths and Flaws of Aaron:

Aaron possessed both strengths and weaknesses that shaped his leadership and service to God and the people of Israel. Some of his strengths include:

- **Loyalty and Support:** Aaron demonstrated loyalty and support to his brother Moses, standing by him in times of challenge and opposition. Despite his initial hesitation, Aaron ultimately obeyed God's call to assist Moses in leading the Israelites out of Egypt.
- **Role as High Priest:** As the first high priest of Israel, Aaron played a pivotal role in mediating between God and the people, offering sacrifices for sin and interceding on behalf of the nation. His consecration as high priest established the priesthood as a central institution in Israelite worship and religious life.
- **Instrument of God's Miracles:** Aaron served as an instrument of God's miracles and signs during the exodus from Egypt, including the turning of the Nile into blood, the plague of frogs, and the parting of the Red Sea. His obedience and cooperation with God's instructions facilitated the deliverance of the Israelites from bondage.

However, Aaron also had his flaws and weaknesses:

- **Complicity in Idolatry:** Despite his role as high priest and mediator between God and the people, Aaron succumbed to pressure from the Israelites and participated in the making of the golden calf at Mount Sinai. His failure to resist the people's demands and uphold God's commandments resulted in divine judgment and loss of credibility as a spiritual leader.
- **Lack of Moral Courage:** Aaron's willingness to compromise his principles and participate in idolatry at the urging of the people revealed a lack of moral courage and spiritual integrity. His fear of displeasing the people outweighed his commitment to obeying God and upholding His holiness. It also showed his lack of trust in God.
- **Failure to Take Responsibility:** After the incident of the golden calf, Aaron attempted to shift the blame onto the people and minimize his own culpability in the sin. His refusal to take full responsibility for his actions further tarnished his reputation as a spiritual leader and undermined his credibility among the people.

God's Response to Aaron:

Despite Aaron's failure and disobedience, God continued to extend mercy and grace to him, reaffirming his role as high priest and mediator between God and the people. Through Moses' intercession, God spared Aaron from immediate judgment and allowed him to continue serving as high priest. However, the incident of the golden calf served as a sobering reminder of the consequences of disobedience and idolatry, both for Aaron and the nation of Israel.

The story of Aaron serves as a cautionary saga about the dangers of compromise and the importance of moral courage and spiritual integrity in leadership. Aaron's failure to resist the people's demands and uphold God's commandments resulted in divine judgment and loss of credibility as a spiritual leader. However, God's grace and mercy remained evident in His continued acceptance of Aaron as high priest and mediator between God and the people. **Please read Exodus 32.**

Conclusion:

Aaron's life serves as a vivid illustration of the complexities and challenges of leadership, particularly in the context of spiritual authority and responsibility. As the first high priest of Israel, Aaron held a position of great honor and influence, tasked with representing the people before God and facilitating their worship and atonement for sin. However, Aaron's actions during the incident of the golden calf reveal the pitfalls and dangers of leadership when motivated by fear, compromise, or the desire for approval from others.

Moreover, Aaron's failure to take responsibility for his actions and his attempt to shift the blame onto the people highlight the importance of humility, transparency, and accountability in leadership. Leaders are called to lead by example, demonstrating integrity, honesty, and a willingness to acknowledge mistakes and seek forgiveness when necessary. Aaron's reluctance to take ownership of his role in the

Brand 316 Inc www.brand316.org 727 North Waco #290 Wichita KS 67203 (316) 247-2050

sin of idolatry only served to erode trust and confidence in his leadership and undermined his effectiveness as a spiritual guide and mediator.

Furthermore, Aaron's story serves as a reminder of the consequences of disobedience and compromise with sin, both for individuals and communities. While God extended mercy and grace to Aaron, allowing him to continue serving as high priest, the repercussions of his actions reverberated throughout Israel's history, contributing to cycles of rebellion, judgment, and restoration. Aaron's failure to uphold God's commands and resist the people's demands resulted in divine discipline and loss of favor, underscoring the importance of obedience and fidelity in our relationship with God. His strengths and weaknesses serve as a sobering reminder of the frailty of human nature and the need for humility and dependence on God's grace.

Aaron's life offers valuable lessons for believers today, reminding us of the importance of moral courage, spiritual integrity, and obedience in our relationship with God and others. His strengths and weaknesses serve as a sobering reminder of the frailty of human nature and the need for humility and dependence on God's grace. As we reflect on Aaron's story, may we be inspired to uphold God's commandments, stand firm in our convictions, and serve Him faithfully in any capacity He calls us to.

Reflective Questions - Answer in Writing

1. In what ways do you see yourself in the strengths and weaknesses of Aaron?

2. Reflect on a time when you were faced with a moral dilemma or pressure to compromise your principles. How did you respond, and what were the consequences of your actions?

3. Consider the importance of moral courage and spiritual integrity in leadership, as exemplified by Aaron. How can we cultivate these qualities in our own lives and spheres of influence?

4. Reflect on Aaron's failure to resist the people's demands and participate in idolatry. How can we guard against the allure of compromise and uphold God's commandments in the face of opposition?

5. How does the story of Aaron challenge you to take responsibility for your actions and strive for obedience and faithfulness in your relationship with God and others?

Week 48: John 3:16 - God's Unconditional Love and Salvation

John 3:16 is one of the most well-known and beloved verses in the Bible. It encapsulates the core message of the Christian faith: God's immense love for humanity and the gift of eternal life through Jesus Christ. It is a significant verse demonstrating God's love and sacrifice!

The Gospel of John

The Gospel of John, written by the Apostle John, presents Jesus as the Son of God and emphasizes His divine nature and mission. It includes profound theological insights and numerous accounts of Jesus' miracles, teachings, and interactions with various individuals.

Immediate Context

John 3:16 is part of a conversation between Jesus and Nicodemus, a Pharisee and a member of the Jewish ruling council. Nicodemus visits Jesus at night, seeking to understand His teachings. Jesus explains the concept of being "born again" and the necessity of spiritual rebirth to enter the Kingdom of God. John 3:16 serves as a summary of Jesus' explanation, highlighting the essence of the Gospel message.

Exploring John 3:16

The Text

"For God so loved the world that he gave his one and only Son, that whoever believes in him shall not perish but have eternal life" (John 3:16, NIV).

Key Phrases

1. **"For God so loved the world"**

   o   This phrase emphasizes the depth and magnitude of God's love for all of humanity, regardless of race, nationality, or status.

2. **"That he gave his one and only Son"**

   o   God's love is demonstrated through the sacrificial gift of His Son, Jesus Christ, who came to earth to save humanity from sin.

3. **"That whoever believes in him"**

   o   Salvation is available to anyone who believes in Jesus as the Son of God, placing their faith and trust in Him.

4. **"Shall not perish but have eternal life"**

   o The promise of eternal life is contrasted with perishing, signifying the difference between everlasting life with God and separation from Him.

Theological Implications

God's Love

John 3:16 highlights the unconditional and sacrificial nature of God's love. It shows that God's love is not limited or exclusive but extends to the entire world.

Jesus' Sacrifice

The verse highlights the significance of Jesus' sacrificial death on the cross. It is through His sacrifice that humanity can receive forgiveness and reconciliation with God.

Faith and Belief

John 3:16 underlines the importance of faith in Jesus for salvation. Belief in Him is the key to receiving eternal life and avoiding spiritual death.

Eternal Life

The promise of eternal life is central to the Christian faith. It assures believers of a future with God, free from the consequences of sin and death.

Practical Applications

Embracing God's Love

Understanding the depth of God's love for us should inspire gratitude and a desire to share that love with others. We can show God's love through acts of kindness, compassion, and forgiveness.

Sharing the Gospel

John 3:16 is a powerful tool for evangelism. It succinctly communicates the core message of the Gospel, making it an excellent verse to share with those seeking to understand Christianity.

Strengthening Our Faith

Reflecting on John 3:16 can strengthen our faith and trust in God. It reminds us of His unwavering love and the incredible sacrifice He made for our salvation.

Living with Hope

The promise of eternal life gives us hope and assurance, even in difficult times. It encourages us to live with an eternal perspective, focusing on our relationship with God and His promises.

Misunderstandings and Cautions

Faith vs. Works

Some may misinterpret John 3:16 to mean that belief alone is sufficient without any change in behavior. While faith is the key to salvation, true belief in Jesus should result in a transformed life characterized by good works and obedience to God's commands.

Universalism

John 3:16 emphasizes that salvation is available to "whoever believes," but it does not imply universal salvation. Only those who place their faith in Jesus will receive eternal life.

Complacency

Knowing the assurance of salvation can sometimes lead to complacency in one's spiritual life. It is important to continually grow in faith, seek God, and live out His teachings.

Biblical Examples

The Conversion of Nicodemus

Nicodemus initially comes to Jesus with questions and doubts. Through his conversation with Jesus, he begins to understand the necessity of spiritual rebirth and the significance of Jesus' mission. Later, Nicodemus shows his faith by assisting in Jesus' burial (John 19:39-40), indicating his transformation.

Modern-Day Believers

Consider a modern-day believer who encounters John 3:16 for the first time. This verse can be a turning point, leading them to accept Jesus as their Savior. Many testimonies reflect how John 3:16 has been instrumental in bringing people to faith, showing its timeless impact. Think about what the verse means to you and the first time you heard it.

Conclusion

John 3:16 is a foundational verse that captures the essence of the Gospel: God's immense love, Jesus' sacrificial mission, the necessity of faith, and the promise of eternal life. By understanding its context, meaning, and practical applications, we can deepen our faith and effectively share this powerful message with others.

As Christians, we are called to embrace God's love, share the Gospel, strengthen our faith, and live with the hope of eternal life. Let us reflect on the profound truths of John 3:16 and allow them to transform our lives, guiding us to live out our faith with gratitude, compassion, and purpose.

Reflective Questions - Answer in Writing

1. What does John 3:16 mean to you?

2. How does John 3:16 challenge your understanding of God's love and salvation?

3. Reflect on a time when you experienced the power of God's love in your life. How did this experience shape your understanding of John 3:16?

4. How does this verse inspire you to live out your faith on a daily basis?

5. How does John 3:16 inspire you to share the message of God's love and salvation with others?

John 4:1-42 recounts the story of Jesus' encounter with the Samaritan woman at the well. It is rich in theological significance and practical application, revealing deep truths about Jesus' mission, the nature of true worship, and the transformative power of the gospel.

The Gospel of John

The Gospel of John presents a unique portrait of Jesus, emphasizing His divine nature and His mission to bring eternal life. John's Gospel is structured around seven signs (miracles) and seven "I Am" statements that reveal Jesus' identity and purpose.

Immediate Context

In John 3, Jesus has a profound conversation with Nicodemus, a Pharisee, about being born again. This sets the stage for His encounter with the Samaritan woman, illustrating that the message of the gospel transcends cultural and social barriers. John 4 contrasts the religious leader's hesitant faith with the Samaritan woman's enthusiastic acceptance of Jesus.

Exploring John 4:1-42

The Text (read the full text in your Bible - John 4:1-42)

Verses 1-6: Setting the Scene

Jesus leaves Judea and travels through Samaria, arriving at Jacob's well around noon. He is tired and sits down by the well while His disciples go into the town to buy food.

Verses 7-15: The Conversation Begins

A Samaritan woman comes to draw water, and Jesus asks her for a drink. She is surprised that He, a Jew, would speak to her, a Samaritan woman. Jesus responds by offering her "living water" that leads to eternal life.

Verses 16-26: Revelation of Jesus' Identity

Jesus reveals His knowledge of her personal life, leading to a conversation about true worship. He declares that true worshipers will worship the Father in spirit and truth. Jesus then reveals Himself as the Messiah.

Verses 27-38: The Disciples' Return and the Harvest

The disciples return and are surprised to find Jesus speaking with the woman. The woman leaves her water jar, goes back to the town, and tells the people about Jesus. Meanwhile, Jesus speaks to His disciples about the spiritual harvest and the importance of laboring for it.

Verses 39-42: The Response of the Samaritans

Many Samaritans from the town believe in Jesus because of the woman's testimony. They invite Jesus to stay with them, and more believe because of His words, acknowledging Him as the Savior.

Key Themes and Phrases

1. **Living Water**

   o   Jesus offers the Samaritan woman "living water," symbolizing eternal life and the Holy Spirit. This water satisfies spiritual thirst and leads to eternal life (John 4:10-14).

2. **True Worship**

   o   Jesus teaches that true worship is not confined to a specific location but is about worshiping the Father in spirit and truth (John 4:23-24).

3. **Revelation of the Messiah**

   o   Jesus reveals Himself as the Messiah to the Samaritan woman, breaking cultural and social barriers (John 4:25-26).

4. **Spiritual Harvest**

   o   Jesus speaks to His disciples about the urgency and importance of the spiritual harvest, emphasizing that the fields are ripe for harvest (John 4:35-38).

Theological Implications

Jesus Breaks Barriers

Jesus' interaction with the Samaritan woman breaks significant social, cultural, and religious barriers. Jews typically avoided Samaritans, and a Jewish man speaking to a Samaritan woman was highly unusual. This encounter illustrates Jesus' mission to reach all people, regardless of their social status.

True Worship

Jesus' teaching on worship emphasizes that true worship is not about location or rituals but about a sincere, heartfelt relationship with God. Worshiping in spirit and truth means worshiping with the right attitude and according to God's revealed truth.

The Role of Testimony

The Samaritan woman's testimony plays a crucial role in leading her townspeople to Jesus. Her immediate and enthusiastic sharing of her encounter with Jesus demonstrates the power of personal testimony in evangelism.

The Urgency of the Harvest

Jesus' conversation with His disciples about the spiritual harvest highlights the urgency of sharing the gospel. The fields are ripe, and there is a need for laborers to bring in the harvest, emphasizing the importance of evangelism and discipleship.

Practical Applications

Sharing the Gospel Across Barriers

- **Be Inclusive**: Reach out to people from different backgrounds, cultures, and social statuses. Follow Jesus' example of breaking barriers and showing love and acceptance to all.

- **Use Your Testimony**: Share your personal experiences of encountering Jesus. Your testimony can be a powerful tool in leading others to faith.

Embracing True Worship

- **Worship with Sincerity**: Focus on worshiping God with a genuine heart. It's not about the external forms but the internal attitude.

- **Seek Truth**: Ground your worship in the truth of God's Word. Study Scripture to understand what true worship entails.

Engaging in the Spiritual Harvest

- **Be Alert**: Recognize the opportunities around you to share the gospel. The fields are ripe for harvest, and there are many people ready to hear about Jesus.

- **Labor Faithfully**: Commit to the work of evangelism and discipleship. Invest time and effort in reaching out to others and helping them grow in their faith.

Misunderstandings and Cautions

Misinterpreting Living Water

Living water represents eternal life and the Holy Spirit. It is not a promise of material prosperity or an easy life but a deep, spiritual fulfillment and relationship with God.

Limiting Worship to Rituals

True worship is not confined to specific rituals or locations. It's about a heartfelt, sincere relationship with God, worshiping Him in spirit and truth.

Biblical Examples

Jesus and Nicodemus

In John 3:1-21, Jesus has a deep theological conversation with Nicodemus, a Pharisee. This contrasts with His more personal and practical conversation with the Samaritan woman, illustrating that the message of the gospel is for everyone, regardless of their background or status.

The Woman Caught in Adultery

In John 8:1-11, Jesus shows mercy and grace to a woman caught in adultery, refusing to condemn her while calling her to repentance. This parallels His compassionate and redemptive approach to the Samaritan woman.

The Ethiopian Eunuch

In Acts 8:26-40, Philip shares the gospel with an Ethiopian eunuch, a foreigner and outcast in Jewish society. This encounter demonstrates the inclusive nature of the gospel and the importance of being led by the Spirit in evangelism.

Conclusion

John 4:1-42 offers a profound and comprehensive narrative that reveals Jesus' mission, the nature of true worship, and the power of personal testimony. Christians can deepen their commitment to sharing the gospel, embracing true worship, and engaging in the spiritual harvest. As Christians, we are called to follow Jesus' example of breaking barriers, worshiping in spirit and truth, and laboring faithfully in the harvest. We should commit to living out these principles in our daily lives, reaching out to others with the love and truth of the gospel, and worshiping God with sincere and genuine hearts.

Reflective Questions – Answer in Writing

1. How does Jesus' interaction with the Samaritan woman challenge your views on reaching out to people from different backgrounds or social statuses?

2. In what ways can you have true worship in your life, focusing on worshiping God in spirit and truth?

3. How can you use your personal testimony to share the gospel with others?

4. What are your top 3 takeaway from this story that can immediately be applied in your life?

5. How is your personal testimony different than most? What are your top 3 experiences that can be used to glorify God and spread the Word – knowing that we serve a God of Second Chances?

Week 50: Luke 4:18–19 - Proclaiming Freedom and Restoration

Luke 4:18-19 is where Jesus announces His mission and ministry. Quoting from the prophet Isaiah, Jesus declares His purpose to bring good news to the poor, proclaim freedom for the prisoners, recovery of sight for the blind, and set the oppressed free. Throughout this study, think about your own life and also that Jesus specifically chose these words and subjects because they matter – you matter and are loved!

The Book of Luke

The Gospel of Luke is one of the four canonical gospels in the New Testament, written by Luke, a physician and companion of Paul. Luke's gospel emphasizes the humanity of Jesus, His compassion for the marginalized and His mission to bring salvation to all people, especially the poor and oppressed.

Immediate Context

Luke 4:18-19 occurs early in Jesus' public ministry. After His baptism and temptation in the wilderness, Jesus returns to Galilee, filled with the Spirit, and begins teaching in synagogues. In Nazareth, His hometown, Jesus stands up to read from the scroll of Isaiah in the synagogue, proclaiming the fulfillment of this prophecy.

Exploring Luke 4:18-19

The Text

"The Spirit of the Lord is on me, because he has anointed me to proclaim good news to the poor. He has sent me to proclaim freedom for the prisoners and recovery of sight for the blind, to set the oppressed free, to proclaim the year of the Lord's favor" (Luke 4:18-19, NIV).

Key Phrases

1. **"The Spirit of the Lord is on me"**

   o This phrase signifies that Jesus' ministry is empowered and guided by the Holy Spirit, emphasizing His divine authority and mission.

2. **"Because he has anointed me"**

   o Anointing signifies being chosen and consecrated for a special mission. Jesus is declaring that He is the Messiah, the Anointed One.

3. **"To proclaim good news to the poor"**

   o The poor, both spiritually and materially, are central to Jesus' mission. He brings hope, salvation, and a new reality to those who are marginalized and in need.

196

4. **"Proclaim freedom for the prisoners"**

   o This phrase indicates liberation from various forms of bondage, including sin, oppression, and physical imprisonment.

5. **"Recovery of sight for the blind"**

   o Jesus' mission includes physical healing as well as spiritual enlightenment, opening the eyes of those who are spiritually blind.

6. **"To set the oppressed free"**

   o Jesus aims to deliver those who are oppressed by various forms of injustice, whether social, economic, or spiritual.

7. **"To proclaim the year of the Lord's favor"**

   o This phrase refers to the Jubilee year, a time of restoration and liberation in Jewish tradition. Jesus is declaring a new era of God's grace and favor.

Theological Implications

Jesus as the Fulfillment of Prophecy

By quoting Isaiah, Jesus identifies Himself as the fulfillment of Old Testament prophecy. He is the long-awaited Messiah who brings God's salvation and liberation to His people.

The Role of the Holy Spirit

The passage highlights the essential role of the Holy Spirit in Jesus' ministry. The Spirit empowers and directs Jesus' mission, indicating that His work is divinely ordained.

A Comprehensive Mission

Jesus' mission is holistic (complete or whole), addressing physical, spiritual, social, and economic needs. He brings good news, healing, liberation, and restoration to all aspects of life.

Practical Applications

Embracing Jesus' Mission

As followers of Christ, we are called to participate in His mission. This involves spreading the gospel, helping the poor, advocating for justice, and bringing healing and hope to those in need.

Empowered by the Holy Spirit

We, too, need the empowerment of the Holy Spirit to fulfill our mission. Regular prayer, seeking the Spirit's guidance, and relying on His power are essential for effective ministry.

Holistic Ministry

Our ministry should reflect Jesus' comprehensive approach. We should address both spiritual and physical needs, working towards holistic transformation in our communities.

Misunderstandings and Cautions

Over-Spiritualizing the Mission

While the spiritual aspects of Jesus' mission are crucial, it's important not to neglect the practical, physical, and social dimensions. Jesus' ministry addresses all aspects of human need.

Ignoring the Role of the Holy Spirit

Attempting to fulfill Jesus' mission in our own strength is useless. We must recognize our dependence on the Holy Spirit for guidance, power, and effectiveness.

Biblical Examples

The Good Samaritan

The parable of the Good Samaritan (Luke 10:25-37) illustrates Jesus' call to compassion and mercy. The Samaritan's care for the injured man exemplifies the kind of holistic, sacrificial love that Jesus' mission embodies.

Zacchaeus

The story of Zacchaeus (Luke 19:1-10) demonstrates the transformative power of Jesus' mission. Zacchaeus, a wealthy tax collector, experiences spiritual and social liberation through his encounter with Jesus, leading to repentance and restitution.

The Woman at the Well

In John 4, Jesus' interaction with the Samaritan woman at the well showcases His mission to bring spiritual enlightenment and liberation. Jesus breaks social barriers and offers her living water, leading to her transformation and the spread of the gospel in her community.

Conclusion

Luke 4:18-19 is a powerful declaration of Jesus' mission and purpose. As Christians, we are called to embrace Jesus' mission, empowered by the Holy Spirit, to bring good news, healing, and liberation to a hurting world. Let us reflect on His compassion, justice, and grace in all aspects of our lives and ministry.

By doing so, we participate in the fulfillment of God's redemptive plan and demonstrate His love and power to those around us.

Reflective Questions - Answer in Writing

1. Read the verses again. What are the two things that standout to you the most and why?

2. Reflect on a time when you experienced God's freedom in life. How has this impacted your perspective on serving others?

3. How can you actively participate in God's mission of freedom and restoration?

4. Why do you think it is important Jesus spoke these words and specifically mentioned "freedom for prisoners." What does that mean to your personally?

5. What steps can you take today to start focusing on these words from Jesus? List out 3 and why they are important.

Week 51: Moses: Faithful Servant of God

The story of Moses is one of courage, faith, and redemption. Despite his flaws and limitations, Moses became one of the greatest leaders in Israel's history, chosen by God to deliver His people from slavery in Egypt. In this lesson, we will explore the life of Moses, examining his strengths, weaknesses, and the ways in which God used him to fulfill His purposes.

Verse to Review: Exodus 3:10

"So now, go. I am sending you to Pharaoh to bring my people the Israelites out of Egypt."

History of Moses:

Moses was born during a time when the Israelites were enslaved in Egypt. Despite being raised as a prince in Pharaoh's court, he was an outsider. Moses identified with his Hebrew heritage and felt called to deliver his people from bondage. After fleeing Egypt following a violent altercation, Moses spent forty years in the wilderness, where God prepared him for his role as Israel's deliverer. At the burning bush, God called Moses to return to Egypt and lead the Israelites to freedom.

Moses's Strengths and Flaws:

Moses possessed several notable strengths, including his deep faith in God and his unwavering commitment to justice. He boldly confronted Pharaoh, demanding the release of the Israelites, and led his people through the wilderness with courage and determination. However, Moses also struggled with feelings of inadequacy and self-doubt. When God initially called him to lead the Israelites, Moses questioned his own abilities and asked God to send someone else in his place (Exodus 3:11, 4:10-13).His insecurity and lack of confidence initially hindered his willingness to obey God's call and step into leadership (Exodus 3:11, 4:10-13).

Moses's temper sometimes got the best of him, leading him to act impulsively and without proper judgment. Moses murdered an Egyptian and then fled the law for 40 years. Another time, iIn a moment of anger, he struck the rock instead of speaking to it as God had commanded; resulting in consequences for himself and his people (Numbers 20:7-12). This incident revealed Moses's struggle to control his emotions and exercise patience in difficult situations.

Also, despite witnessing God's faithfulness and miraculous power firsthand, Moses sometimes struggled to fully trust and obey God's commands. When faced with challenges or uncertainties, he occasionally questioned God's guidance and made decisions based on his own understanding rather than God's direction (Exodus 5:22-23, Numbers 14:1-4).

God's Redemption Through Moses's Faith:

Despite Moses's flaws and limitations, God remained faithful to His promise and used Moses to accomplish His purposes. Through Moses, God brought about the miraculous deliverance of the Israelites from slavery in Egypt, demonstrating His power and sovereignty over the nations. Despite Moses's initial reluctance, he ultimately embraced his role as God's chosen leader and faithfully led the Israelites through the wilderness to the edge of the Promised Land.

Conclusion:

Moses's journey from reluctant leader to faithful servant is a remarkable testament to God's grace and power. Despite his initial hesitation and self-doubt, Moses ultimately embraced his calling and led the Israelites with courage and conviction. His story serves as an inspiration to all who are called to step out in faith and obedience, trusting in God's provision and guidance every step of the way.

One of the most significant challenges Moses faced was his struggle with feelings of inadequacy and self-doubt. Despite being chosen by God for a monumental task, Moses questioned his own abilities and qualifications to lead the Israelites out of Egypt. His insecurity and fear of failure initially hindered his willingness to obey God's call and step into the role of deliverer. However, God patiently reassured Moses of His presence and power, equipping him with everything he needed to fulfill his mission.

Moses's impulsive actions, particularly his outburst of anger at the rock in the wilderness, serve as a cautionary tale about the dangers of allowing emotions to dictate our behavior. In a moment of frustration and impatience, Moses struck the rock instead of speaking to it as God had commanded, resulting in consequences for himself and his people. This incident revealed Moses's struggle to control his temper and exercise patience in difficult situations, reminding us of the importance of self-control and humility in our own lives. He had this issue early in his life when he murdered the Egyptian.

Despite his flaws and shortcomings, Moses's faithfulness and obedience ultimately paved the way for the fulfillment of God's promises to His people. Through Moses, God demonstrated His power and sovereignty over the nations, bringing about the miraculous deliverance of the Israelites from slavery in Egypt and leading them through the wilderness. Moses's leadership was characterized by his trust in God's guidance and his commitment to following His commands, even in the face of seemingly insurmountable obstacles.

Despite Moses having several flaws and poor choices, God still used him for His glory. It is important to think about your situation and reflect on the fact that God has the power to fully change everything. The important step is focusing on Him and giving Him your life.

Moses's life is a testament to the transformative power of faith and obedience. Despite his flaws and weaknesses, God used Moses to accomplish His purposes and bring about the deliverance of His people. We have to trust in God's faithfulness and step out in obedience to His call, knowing that He is able to use even the most unlikely individuals to fulfill His plans.

Reflective Questions - Answer in Writing

1. In what areas of your life do you struggle with feelings of inadequacy or self-doubt, like Moses did?

2. Reflect on a time when God called you to step out in faith and obedience. How did you respond? What did you learn from that experience?

3. Consider the consequences of Moses's impulsive actions, particularly when he struck the rock instead of speaking to it as God had commanded. How can we learn from his example in our own lives?

4. Despite his flaws, God still used Moses to accomplish His purposes. How does this give you hope for your own life, despite your imperfections?

5. How can you cultivate a deeper sense of trust and obedience in God's guidance, even when faced with challenges or uncertainties?

Luke 23:42-43 captures a poignant moment during the crucifixion of Jesus, highlighting the promise of salvation and the power of faith even in the final moments of life. This story shows depth of Christ's mercy and the assurance of eternal life highlighting that we truly do serve a God of second chances.

The Gospel of Luke

The Gospel of Luke is one of the four Gospels in the New Testament, known for its detailed narrative and emphasis on Jesus' compassion and inclusivity. Luke, a physician and companion of Paul, wrote this Gospel to provide an orderly account of Jesus' life, ministry, death, and resurrection.

Immediate Context

In Luke 23, Jesus is crucified alongside two criminals. As He endures the agony of the cross, various people mock Him, but one of the criminals recognizes Jesus' innocence and divinity. This interaction occurs during Jesus' final hours, emphasizing His role as Savior even in His suffering.

Exploring Luke 23:42-43

The Text

"Then he said, 'Jesus, remember me when you come into your kingdom.' Jesus answered him, 'Truly I tell you, today you will be with me in paradise'" (Luke 23:42-43, NIV).

Key Phrases

1. **"Jesus, remember me when you come into your kingdom"**

   o This statement is a profound expression of faith. The criminal acknowledges Jesus as the Messiah and believes in His kingdom despite the circumstances.

2. **"Truly I tell you"**

   o Jesus' response begins with an affirmation of truth, underlining the certainty of His promise.

3. **"Today you will be with me in paradise"**

   o Jesus assures the criminal that he will join Him in paradise immediately after death, highlighting the immediacy of salvation and the promise of eternal life.

Theological Implications

Brand 316 Inc www.brand316.org 727 North Waco #290 Wichita KS 67203 (316) 247-2050

The Power of Faith

The criminal's request demonstrates that even a simple, sincere faith in Jesus is sufficient for salvation. Despite his past, his belief in Jesus' identity and kingdom grants him eternal life.

The Assurance of Salvation

Jesus' promise to the criminal provides a powerful assurance of salvation. It underscores that salvation is not based on works or merit but on faith in Christ and His grace.

The Compassion of Christ

Even in His suffering, Jesus extends mercy and compassion. His willingness to forgive and save the criminal reflects His boundless love and grace.

Practical Applications

Embracing Simple Faith

Recognize that salvation comes through faith in Jesus Christ. Embrace the simplicity and power of trusting in Jesus, regardless of your past or circumstances.

Offering Assurance to Others

Share the message of assurance that salvation is available to all who believe in Jesus. Encourage others to place their faith in Him and experience the promise of eternal life.

Demonstrating Christ's Compassion

Reflect Jesus' compassion in your interactions with others. Extend grace, forgiveness, and love, especially to those who are struggling or facing difficult circumstances.

Misunderstandings and Cautions

Misinterpreting the Timing of Salvation

Some may misinterpret Jesus' promise as indicating that paradise is immediate for everyone. Understand that Jesus' statement was specific to the criminal's faith and circumstance, but it does affirm the immediacy of salvation for believers.

Overlooking the Depth of Repentance

While the criminal's faith was simple, it also involved recognition of his own sin and a turning towards Jesus. Emphasize the importance of repentance as a component of genuine faith.

Neglecting the Transformative Power of Salvation

Salvation is not just a promise for the afterlife but also a transformative power for our present lives. Encourage others to live out their faith and allow it to shape their actions and relationships.

Biblical Examples

The Thief on the Cross

The criminal's interaction with Jesus (Luke 23:39-43) serves as a direct case study. His recognition of Jesus' divinity, his repentance, and his faith illustrate the core elements of salvation.

Zacchaeus

In Luke 19:1-10, Zacchaeus, a tax collector, encounters Jesus and experiences transformation. His faith leads to repentance and restitution, demonstrating the immediate and transformative power of salvation.

The Woman at the Well

In John 4:1-26, Jesus interacts with a Samaritan woman, offering her living water. Her faith in Jesus leads to a changed life and the spread of the Gospel in her community, highlighting the inclusivity and transformative power of salvation.

Conclusion

Luke 23:42-43 offers a sincere glimpse into the promise of salvation through faith in Jesus Christ. As Christians, we are called to embrace simple faith, offer assurance to others, and demonstrate Christ's compassion. Let us focus on living out our faith with the confidence of salvation and the transformative power of God's grace. By doing so, we reflect the hope and promise of eternal life that Jesus offers to all who believe.

Reflective Questions – Answer in Writing

1. How does the interaction between Jesus and the criminal on the cross impact your understanding of salvation through faith?

2. In what ways can you offer assurance and hope of salvation to those around you?

3. Reflect on a time when you experienced or witnessed Christ's compassion. How can you demonstrate that same compassion to others?

4. How does the immediacy of the criminal's salvation challenge or encourage you in your own faith journey?

5. What steps can you take to live out the transformative power of salvation in your daily life?

Appendix A: Tactics for Effective Scripture Memorization

1. Choose Meaningful Verses

Select verses that resonate with you personally or address specific areas of your life. When a verse holds personal significance, you are more likely to remember it. Start with well-known passages and gradually expand to other parts of Scripture. Verses that provide comfort, guidance, or conviction are excellent choices.

2. Use Repetition

Repetition is key to memorization. Write the verse on a card or in a notebook and repeat it aloud several times a day. Review it regularly, especially in the first few days. Consistent repetition helps transfer the verse from short-term to long-term memory.

3. Break It Down

Divide longer verses or passages into smaller, manageable sections. Focus on memorizing one section at a time, then gradually combine them. This method makes it less overwhelming and allows for more focused retention.

4. Engage Multiple Senses

Utilize different senses to reinforce memory. Write the verse down, read it aloud, and listen to it. Visual learners can benefit from seeing the verse, auditory learners from hearing it, and kinesthetic learners from writing it. Engaging multiple senses strengthens the memorization process.

5. Create Associations

Associate the verse with a visual image, a specific location, or a personal experience. For example, if you're memorizing Psalm 1:3, picture a tree planted by streams of water. Associations create mental hooks that make the verse easier to recall.

6. Use Mnemonic Devices

Mnemonic devices, such as acronyms or rhymes, can aid memorization. For example, to remember Philippians 4:6 ("Do not be anxious about anything, but in every situation, by prayer and petition, with thanksgiving, present your requests to God"), you might create an acronym like "AAPT" (Anxious, Anything, Prayer, Thanksgiving).

7. Practice Recitation

Regularly recite the verse from memory. Test yourself by covering the written text and trying to recall the verse. Recitation reinforces retention and highlights areas that need more practice.

8. Incorporate into Prayer

Incorporate the verse into your prayers. Praying Scripture not only reinforces memorization but also deepens your spiritual connection to the verse. For example, if you're memorizing James 1:5 ("If any of you lacks wisdom, you should ask God"), incorporate it into your prayers for guidance.

9. Find a Memorization Partner

Partner with a friend or family member for mutual accountability and encouragement. Share the verses you're memorizing and recite them to each other. A memorization partner provides motivation and support.

10. Meditate on the Verse

Meditation involves deeply thinking about the verse and its meaning. Spend time reflecting on the verse, considering its context, and pondering its application to your life. Meditation enhances understanding and retention.

11. Incorporate into Daily Life

Integrate the memorized verses into your daily activities. Display them in places you frequently see, such as on your bathroom mirror, locker, or cell door. The more you encounter the verses, the more ingrained they become.

Appendix B: Old Testament Book Summaries

1. **Genesis**

   o **Summary**: Genesis, the first book of the Bible, covers the creation of the world, the fall of humanity, the flood, and the patriarchs Abraham, Isaac, Jacob, and Joseph. It traces the origins of the universe, sin, and God's covenant relationship with humanity. Genesis ends with the Israelites living in Egypt under Joseph's protection.

2. **Exodus**

   o **Summary**: Exodus recounts the Israelites' enslavement in Egypt, their deliverance through Moses, and their journey to Mount Sinai. It includes the ten plagues, the crossing of the Red Sea, the giving of the Ten Commandments, and the instructions for building the Tabernacle. It highlights God's redemption and His covenant with Israel.

3. **Leviticus**

   o **Summary**: Leviticus contains laws and regulations for worship, sacrifices, and holy living for the Israelites. It emphasizes holiness, the role of the priesthood, and the importance of atonement and ritual purity. Key themes include the Day of Atonement and various festivals.

4. **Numbers**

   o **Summary**: Numbers records the Israelites' wilderness wanderings from Mount Sinai to the plains of Moab. It includes census data, laws, and narratives of rebellion and punishment. The book highlights God's guidance, provision, and discipline, as well as the preparation for entering the Promised Land.

5. **Deuteronomy**

   o **Summary**: Deuteronomy is Moses' farewell address to the Israelites, reiterating the law and renewing the covenant. It emphasizes obedience, loyalty to God, and the blessings and curses associated with following or forsaking the covenant. It concludes with Moses' death and the transition of leadership to Joshua.

6. **Joshua**

- Summary: Joshua recounts the conquest and settlement of the Promised Land under Joshua's leadership. It includes the crossing of the Jordan River, the fall of Jericho, and the division of the land among the tribes of Israel. The book emphasizes God's faithfulness and the importance of obedience.

7. **Judges**

- Summary: Judges chronicles the cycle of Israel's sin, oppression, deliverance, and relapse during the time of the judges. Key figures include Deborah, Gideon, and Samson. The book highlights the consequences of Israel's disobedience and the need for righteous leadership.

8. **Ruth**

- Summary: Ruth tells the story of a Moabite woman who remains loyal to her Israelite mother-in-law, Naomi, and becomes the great-grandmother of King David. The book emphasizes themes of loyalty, kindness, and God's providence. It shows God's inclusion of Gentiles in His redemptive plan.

9. **1 Samuel**

- Summary: 1 Samuel recounts the transition from the period of judges to the monarchy in Israel. It covers the life of Samuel, the rise and fall of King Saul, and the anointing of David as king. The book highlights themes of leadership, obedience, and God's sovereignty.

10. **2 Samuel**

- Summary: 2 Samuel focuses on the reign of King David, including his military victories, establishment of Jerusalem as the capital, and his covenant with God. It also addresses David's moral failures, family strife, and the rebellion of Absalom. The book underscores the complexities of leadership and God's enduring promises.

11. **1 Kings**

- Summary: 1 Kings details the reign of Solomon, the division of the kingdom into Israel (north) and Judah (south), and the subsequent kings of both kingdoms. It highlights Solomon's wisdom, the construction of the Temple, and the spiritual decline leading to the prophetic ministries of Elijah and Elisha.

12. **2 Kings**

- Summary: 2 Kings continues the history of the divided kingdoms, documenting the decline and fall of both Israel and Judah. Key events include the ministries of Elijah and

Elisha, the Assyrian conquest of Israel, and the Babylonian exile of Judah. The book emphasizes the consequences of idolatry and disobedience.

13. **1 Chronicles**

   o **Summary**: 1 Chronicles retells the history of Israel from Adam to the death of King David, with a focus on David's reign. It includes genealogies, David's military exploits, and preparations for the Temple. The book emphasizes Davidic kingship and the centrality of worship.

14. **2 Chronicles**

   o **Summary**: 2 Chronicles continues the history of Israel, focusing on the reign of Solomon and the kings of Judah until the Babylonian exile. It highlights the construction and dedication of the Temple, the reforms of righteous kings, and the consequences of unfaithfulness. The book emphasizes the importance of true worship and adherence to God's laws.

15. **Ezra**

   o **Summary**: Ezra recounts the return of the Jewish exiles from Babylon, the rebuilding of the Temple, and the spiritual reforms led by Ezra. It emphasizes God's faithfulness in restoring His people and the importance of obedience to the Torah. Key events include the opposition to the rebuilding efforts and the renewal of the covenant.

16. **Nehemiah**

   o **Summary**: Nehemiah continues the story of the return from exile, focusing on the rebuilding of Jerusalem's walls under Nehemiah's leadership. It highlights themes of perseverance, prayer, and community reform. Nehemiah's efforts to restore the city and its people reflect God's ongoing work in rebuilding and renewing His people.

17. **Esther**

   o **Summary**: Esther tells the story of a Jewish woman who becomes queen of Persia and saves her people from a genocidal plot. The book highlights themes of providence, courage, and divine deliverance. Despite the absence of direct references to God, His hand is evident in the unfolding events.

18. **Job**

   o **Summary**: Job explores the nature of suffering and God's sovereignty through the story of Job, a righteous man who endures intense suffering. It includes dialogues between Job and his friends, who debate the reasons for his afflictions, and God's response,

Brand 316 Inc www.brand316.org 727 North Waco #290 Wichita KS 67203 (316) 247-2050

which highlights His wisdom and power. The book addresses the complexities of faith and suffering.

19. **Psalms**

   o **Summary**: Psalms is a collection of 150 songs, prayers, and poems that express a wide range of emotions, from praise and thanksgiving to lament and supplication. Written by various authors, including David, the Psalms address themes of worship, trust, and the human experience. They serve as a guide for personal and communal prayer and worship.

20. **Proverbs**

   o **Summary**: Proverbs is a collection of wise sayings and instructions for living a righteous and prudent life. Attributed primarily to Solomon, the book emphasizes the fear of the Lord as the foundation of wisdom. It covers various topics, including work, relationships, speech, and moral conduct.

21. **Ecclesiastes**

   o **Summary**: Ecclesiastes, attributed to Solomon, reflects on the meaning and purpose of life. The author, referred to as the Teacher, explores the futility of human endeavors and the transient nature of life. The book concludes with a call to fear God and keep His commandments as the ultimate duty of humanity.

22. **Song of Solomon**

   o **Summary**: Song of Solomon is a poetic and allegorical celebration of love between a bride and groom. It explores themes of love, desire, and the beauty of marital intimacy. The book is often interpreted as an allegory of God's love for His people or Christ's love for the Church.

23. **Isaiah**

   o **Summary**: Isaiah contains prophecies of judgment and salvation, addressing the sins of Judah, Israel, and the nations. It includes messages of hope and the coming of the Messiah, known as the "Suffering Servant." The book emphasizes God's holiness, justice, and redemptive plan for His people.

24. **Jeremiah**

   o **Summary**: Jeremiah records the prophecies of Jeremiah, who warned Judah of impending judgment and urged repentance. It includes messages of doom, personal

212

struggles, and promises of restoration. The book highlights God's patience and the inevitability of His judgment due to persistent sin.

25. Lamentations

- o **Summary**: Lamentations is a collection of poetic laments mourning the destruction of Jerusalem and the Temple by the Babylonians. Attributed to Jeremiah, the book expresses grief, sorrow, and repentance. It also contains expressions of hope in God's faithfulness and mercy.

26. Ezekiel

- o **Summary**: Ezekiel contains the prophecies and visions of Ezekiel, who ministered to the exiles in Babylon. It includes messages of judgment against Israel and the nations, and promises of restoration. Key themes include the glory of God, the new covenant, and the future Temple.

27. Daniel

- o **Summary**: Daniel recounts the experiences of Daniel and his friends in Babylon, including their faithfulness in the face of persecution. It also contains apocalyptic visions of future kingdoms and the end times. The book emphasizes God's sovereignty over history and His deliverance of the faithful.

28. Hosea

- o **Summary**: Hosea uses the prophet's troubled marriage to symbolize God's relationship with unfaithful Israel. It contains messages of judgment and hope, emphasizing God's love and mercy despite Israel's infidelity. Hosea's life and prophecies illustrate God's desire for repentance and restoration.

29. Joel

- o **Summary**: Joel addresses a devastating locust plague in Judah and calls for national repentance. It includes prophecies of the "Day of the Lord" and the outpouring of the Holy Spirit. The book emphasizes God's sovereignty, judgment, and the promise of restoration.

30. Amos

- o **Summary**: Amos delivers messages of judgment against Israel and the surrounding nations for their injustices and idolatry. It emphasizes social justice, righteousness, and God's disdain for empty religious rituals. The book calls for genuine repentance and moral integrity.

31. Obadiah

- o **Summary**: Obadiah is the shortest book in the Old Testament, prophesying the downfall of Edom for their pride and mistreatment of Israel. It emphasizes God's justice and the restoration of Israel. The book highlights the consequences of arrogance and hostility towards God's people.

32. Jonah

- o **Summary**: Jonah recounts the story of the reluctant prophet who is sent to warn Nineveh of impending judgment. After initially fleeing, Jonah obeys, and the city repents. The book highlights God's compassion and mercy for all people, even those outside Israel.

33. Micah

- o **Summary**: Micah delivers messages of judgment and hope, addressing the sins of Israel and Judah. It includes prophecies of the Messiah's birth in Bethlehem and the establishment of God's kingdom. The book emphasizes justice, mercy, and humble obedience to God.

34. Nahum

- o **Summary**: Nahum prophesies the fall of Nineveh, the capital of Assyria, for their cruelty and wickedness. It emphasizes God's justice and the certainty of His judgment against oppressive nations. The book provides comfort to those who suffer under tyranny.

35. Habakkuk

- o **Summary**: Habakkuk dialogues with God about the problem of evil and the coming judgment on Judah by the Babylonians. It includes expressions of faith and trust in God's sovereignty. The book emphasizes living by faith and finding hope in God's ultimate justice.

36. Zephaniah

- o **Summary**: Zephaniah warns of the coming "Day of the Lord," a time of judgment for Judah and the nations. It includes calls for repentance and promises of restoration. The book highlights God's holiness, justice, and the hope of a purified remnant.

37. Haggai

o **Summary**: Haggai encourages the returned exiles to rebuild the Temple in Jerusalem. It emphasizes the importance of prioritizing God's work and promises blessings for obedience. The book highlights God's presence and the future glory of the Temple.

38. Zechariah

o **Summary**: Zechariah contains visions and prophecies encouraging the exiles to complete the Temple and look forward to the coming Messiah. It includes themes of spiritual renewal, God's protection, and the ultimate triumph of God's kingdom. The book emphasizes hope and restoration.

39. Malachi

o **Summary**: Malachi addresses the spiritual apathy and moral lapses of the returned exiles. It includes calls for sincere worship, faithful stewardship, and the coming "Day of the Lord." The book highlights God's love, justice, and the promise of a messenger to prepare the way for the Messiah.

Appendix C: New Testament Book Summaries

1. **Matthew**

   o **Summary**: The Gospel of Matthew presents Jesus as the long-awaited Messiah and King of the Jews. It begins with a genealogy linking Jesus to Abraham and David, followed by an account of His birth, ministry, teachings (including the Sermon on the Mount), miracles, death, and resurrection. Matthew emphasizes Jesus' fulfillment of Old Testament prophecies and His authority as a teacher and healer.

2. **Mark**

   o **Summary**: The Gospel of Mark is the shortest and most action-packed of the four Gospels. It portrays Jesus as the suffering servant and Son of God. Mark focuses on Jesus' deeds more than His teachings, highlighting His miracles, exorcisms, and authoritative acts. The book ends abruptly with the empty tomb, emphasizing the resurrection and the call to discipleship.

3. **Luke**

   o **Summary**: The Gospel of Luke provides a detailed and orderly account of Jesus' life, emphasizing His compassion and care for the marginalized. Luke highlights Jesus' parables, His interactions with sinners, and His journey to Jerusalem. The book also includes the birth narratives of both John the Baptist and Jesus, and concludes with Jesus' ascension.

4. **John**

   o **Summary**: The Gospel of John focuses on the divine nature of Jesus, presenting Him as the eternal Word (Logos) who became flesh. John's Gospel includes seven "I Am" statements and seven signs (miracles) that reveal Jesus' identity and mission. It emphasizes belief in Jesus for eternal life and includes extended discourses, such as the Farewell Discourse and the High Priestly Prayer.

5. **Acts**

   o **Summary**: The Acts of the Apostles, written by Luke, narrates the history of the early church from Jesus' ascension to Paul's imprisonment in Rome. It details the outpouring of the Holy Spirit at Pentecost, the spread of the gospel through the apostles, the conversion of Saul (Paul), and the missionary journeys of Paul. Acts highlights the growth of the church and the challenges it faced.

6. **Romans**

   o **Summary**: Romans, written by Paul, is a comprehensive theological treatise that explains the righteousness of God, justification by faith, and the implications for both Jews and Gentiles. It covers themes such as sin, salvation, sanctification, and the sovereignty of God. Paul exhorts believers to live transformed lives in light of the gospel.

7. **1 Corinthians**

   o **Summary**: In 1 Corinthians, Paul addresses various issues within the Corinthian church, including divisions, immorality, and confusion over spiritual gifts. He provides instructions on marriage, the Lord's Supper, and the resurrection. The famous "love chapter" (1 Corinthians 13) emphasizes the supremacy of love in the Christian life.

8. **2 Corinthians**

   o **Summary**: 2 Corinthians is a deeply personal letter in which Paul defends his apostleship and expresses his love for the Corinthians. He discusses his sufferings, the ministry of reconciliation, and the collection for the Jerusalem church. Paul contrasts the old and new covenants and highlights the power of God in weakness.

9. **Galatians**

   o **Summary**: Galatians is Paul's vigorous defense of the gospel of grace against the Judaizers, who insisted that Gentile Christians must follow the Mosaic Law. Paul emphasizes justification by faith apart from the works of the law and the freedom believers have in Christ. He contrasts the works of the flesh with the fruit of the Spirit.

10. **Ephesians**

    o **Summary**: Ephesians highlights the spiritual blessings believers have in Christ, the unity of the church, and the mystery of the gospel. Paul discusses themes such as election, redemption, and the church as the body of Christ. He provides practical instructions for living out the Christian faith in relationships, work, and spiritual warfare.

11. **Philippians**

    o **Summary**: Philippians is a joyful letter written by Paul from prison, encouraging the believers to rejoice in the Lord. He emphasizes the importance of humility, unity, and perseverance in the faith. Paul highlights Christ's example of humility and obedience and exhorts the Philippians to shine as lights in the world.

12. **Colossians**

- Summary: In Colossians, Paul addresses false teachings that threatened the church and emphasizes the supremacy and sufficiency of Christ. He highlights the preeminence of Christ in creation, redemption, and the church. Paul provides practical instructions for Christian living, urging believers to set their minds on things above.

13. **1 Thessalonians**

- Summary: 1 Thessalonians is a letter of encouragement and instruction, written by Paul to the young church in Thessalonica. He commends their faith, love, and hope, and provides teachings on holy living and the return of Christ. Paul reassures the believers about the fate of those who have died in Christ and encourages them to remain steadfast.

14. **2 Thessalonians**

- Summary: In 2 Thessalonians, Paul addresses misunderstandings about the second coming of Christ and warns against idleness. He provides further teaching on the end times, the man of lawlessness, and the importance of standing firm in the faith. Paul exhorts the believers to work diligently and live orderly lives.

15. **1 Timothy**

- Summary: 1 Timothy is a pastoral letter written by Paul to his young protégé, Timothy. It provides instructions on church leadership, sound doctrine, and godly living. Paul addresses issues such as false teaching, qualifications for church leaders, and the roles of men and women in the church. He encourages Timothy to be a faithful and courageous pastor.

16. **2 Timothy**

- Summary: 2 Timothy is Paul's final letter, written from prison as he faces imminent execution. It is a personal and emotional letter, urging Timothy to remain faithful to the gospel and to endure hardships. Paul emphasizes the importance of Scripture, the need for perseverance, and the reward awaiting those who remain faithful to the end.

17. **Titus**

- Summary: Titus is a pastoral letter written by Paul to Titus, who was overseeing the churches on the island of Crete. Paul provides instructions on appointing church leaders, teaching sound doctrine, and promoting good works. He emphasizes the importance of living godly lives and being a witness to the surrounding culture.

18. **Philemon**

- Summary: Philemon is a personal letter from Paul to Philemon, a wealthy Christian in Colossae. Paul appeals to Philemon to welcome back his runaway slave, Onesimus, who has become a believer. Paul emphasizes forgiveness, reconciliation, and the transformation that the gospel brings to relationships.

19. **Hebrews**

- Summary: Hebrews is a theological treatise that presents Jesus as the superior and final revelation of God. The author contrasts Jesus with angels, Moses, the high priests, and the sacrificial system, emphasizing His superiority. The book encourages believers to hold fast to their faith and warns against apostasy, highlighting the importance of perseverance.

20. **James**

- Summary: James is a practical letter that emphasizes the importance of living out one's faith through actions. James addresses issues such as trials, wisdom, speech, wealth, and prayer. He stresses that genuine faith produces good works and calls believers to live lives of integrity and compassion.

21. **1 Peter**

- Summary: 1 Peter is a letter of encouragement to believers facing persecution. Peter reminds them of their living hope in Christ, the importance of holy living, and their identity as God's chosen people. He exhorts them to endure suffering with faith and to be a witness to the world through their conduct.

22. **2 Peter**

- Summary: 2 Peter is a letter warning against false teachers and emphasizing the importance of growing in the knowledge of Christ. Peter encourages believers to live godly lives and to be diligent in their faith. He reminds them of the certainty of Christ's return and the coming judgment.

23. **1 John**

- Summary: 1 John is a pastoral letter that emphasizes the importance of love, obedience, and truth. John addresses issues of false teaching, assuring believers of their salvation and encouraging them to live in fellowship with God and one another. He highlights the themes of light and darkness, love and hate, and truth and error.

24. **2 John**

- Summary: 2 John is a brief letter emphasizing the importance of walking in truth and love. John warns against false teachers who deny the incarnation of Christ and instructs the recipients to avoid those who do not adhere to sound doctrine. He encourages them to remain faithful to the teachings of Christ.

25. **3 John**

- Summary: 3 John is a personal letter to Gaius, commending him for his hospitality and faithfulness to the truth. John contrasts Gaius with Diotrephes, who seeks to dominate the church and rejects John's authority. He encourages Gaius to continue doing good and to support those who work for the gospel.

26. **Jude**

- Summary: Jude is a short letter warning against false teachers who have infiltrated the church. Jude urges believers to contend for the faith and to be vigilant against those who pervert the grace of God. He reminds them of God's judgment on the ungodly and encourages them to build themselves up in the faith.

27. **Revelation**

- Summary: The Book of Revelation is a prophetic and apocalyptic book written by the Apostle John. It contains visions of the end times, the final judgment, and the ultimate victory of Christ over evil. The book addresses the seven churches of Asia, describes the tribulation, the second coming of Christ, the millennium, the final judgment, and the new heaven and new earth. Revelation provides hope and encouragement to believers, assuring them of Christ's return and the establishment of His eternal kingdom.

 **316**

APPLY TODAY!

Brand 316, Inc is a Christian ministry focused on preparing you for success while in prison and immediately after release. The program is FREE! Apply Today

Brand 316 focuses on the **core issues causing recidivism** through real world career and reintegration training, preparation, accountability, immediate employment, housing, a strong Christian support network and a path to success while bringing Glory to God. **Throughout the Bible, God uses our failures for His Glory!** 68% of inmates are rearrested within 3 years after release. The odds are not in your favor unless you make the effort now to realistically **prepare** for your future **after** prison. Decide on success!

Problems Faced	The Brand 316 Solution
o **Employment**: National Recidivism Rate is 68%. 85% of those rearrested were unemployed. The recidivism rate for the employed was only 9%!	✓ Provide immediate employment upon release ✓ 12 month personalized job training ✓ Career placement upon graduation
o **Hopelessness**: Majority of the formerly incarcerated **expect** to be back in jail eventually.	✓ Provide a Strong x Consistent support network ✓ 12 month reintegration training and support
o **Housing:** Without a family or friends house, the answer is the streets or a shelter	✓ Partner with several local housing options ✓ Immediate Housing upon release
o **Transportation:** Getting to and from work, church and other obligations	✓ Match local employment and churches ✓ Provide realistic options and approaches
o **Poverty:** Incarceration has increased the U.S. poverty rate by an estimated 20%.	✓ Reducing recidivism reduces poverty – a direct calling for all to focus on
o **Society and Churches Perceptions:** Fear, untrustworthy, unwillingness to forgive and move on, little can be done to help, not our problem.	✓ 1 of 4 Americans has a criminal record ✓ Change perceptions through actions and info ✓ God Uses our past failures for His Glory
o **Reintegration:** Success or failure depends on preparation focused on creating positive habits, knowledge, realistic expectations x education.	✓ Training and preparation for 2-4 years in Prison ✓ 12 month reintegration program upon release focused on successful reintegration into society
o **Career Training:** A job is short term, a career is focusing on the long term and developing the habits x skills needed to succeed professionally.	✓ Realistic employment training and goals focused on skills development, real world situational training, education, aptitude tests and more

- Preparation for release from prison while inside including training materials, communication, study guides, workbooks, etc. Includes personalized release plan.
- 52 week personalized career training upon release preparing you for long term success.
- 52 week intense reintegration training to help you succeed in everyday life and thrive.
- Weekly Bible Studies, Mentorship & Commitment to Church. **Christ first in all we do!**

A Realistic Path to Long Term Success - Apply For Brand 316 today!

Several Ways to Request an Application
• Add us to your email and email us at david@brand316.org.
• Have your family request an application for you on our website. www.brand316.org
• Mail us a letter requesting it: 727 N. Waco Ave #290 Wichita KS 67203
• Call us at (316) 247-2050 and leave a message.
When you contact us: Please provide your full name, id number, prison location and your expected release date and we will immediately mail your application!

Brand 316 Inc www.brand316.org 727 North Waco #290 Wichita KS 67203 (316) 247-2050

Made in the USA
Monee, IL
07 August 2024

63471223R00122